No. 3235 Payne Bluff, K. & S. Ry. near Sandon, B C.

BRITISH COLUMBIA
100 YEARS AGO

Portraits of a Province

Fred Thirkell and Bob Scullion

Copyright © 2002 Fred Thirkell and Bob Scullion

National Library of Canada Cataloguing in Publication Data

Thirkell, Fred, 1930-
    British Columbia 100 years ago

    Includes bibliographical references and index.
    ISBN 1-894384-49-0 (bound). —ISBN 1-894384-50-4 (pbk.)

    1. British Columbia—History—1871-1918—Pictorial works. 2. Postcards—British Columbia.
I. Scullion, Bob, 1937-   II. Title. III. Title: British Columbia one hundred years ago.

FC3812.T44 2002   971.1'03'0222   C2002-910908-6
F1087.8.T44 2002

First edition 2002

Heritage House acknowledges the financial support for our publishing program from the Government of Canada through the Book Publishing Industry Development Program (BPIDP), Canada Council for the Arts, and the British Columbia Arts Council.

Edited by Judith Brand and Vivian Sinclair
Book design by Bob Scullion
Cover design by Darlene Nickull

HERITAGE HOUSE PUBLISHING COMPANY LTD.
Unit #108 - 17665 66 A Ave., Surrey, B.C. V3S 2A7

Printed in Canada

TABLE OF CONTENTS

ACKNOWLEDGEMENTS

Sincere thanks go to all those who have made the publication of *British Columbia 100 Years Ago* possible. As always, we acknowledge with thanks the people who staff our local libraries and archives. Whether professionals or volunteers, those who work so hard to preserve the history of our province deserve much more recognition than they generally receive. We particularly want to say thanks for the assistance provided by Barbara Girvan and her staff at the Revelstoke Railway Museum; it has been most helpful.

We are grateful for the assistance provided by John Davies, Richard Moulton, and John Pitt, who generously allowed us to reproduce postcards from their collections. It is not stretching the truth to say that without the help of these three collectors, *British Columbia 100 Years Ago* could not have come to be. As well, a word of thanks goes to the people at Heritage House—our publisher, Rodger Touchie; our editors, Judith Brand and Vivian Sinclair; the firm's production manager, Darlene Nickull; and Karen Berreth and Diane Komorowski, who are always so accommodating and helpful.

And as always, we thank those on the home front—Lil Thirkell and Beth Fish—for their continuing patience and useful advice. While on occasion their criticism may not have been immediately appreciated, it was invariably right on!

PREFACE

British Columbia 100 Years Ago is our fifth book that sets out to say something about British Columbia's past. Readers already familiar with our unique (some call it, peculiar) approach to our province's history know that we always begin with visual images—in this instance printed postcards—that for one reason or another have a special appeal. We then write pieces that say something about the pictures chosen.

As always, we set out to do a number of things. First of all, we aim to produce a book that is attractive and visually appealing. We appreciate the fact that our publisher allows us the freedom not only to determine content, but also the layout and format for our books. We also hope to inform without being patronizing. If as a reader you are able to say at some point, "I didn't know that," with a note of pleasant surprise in your voice, then we have succeeded on that count. But it is not enough to surprise; we also hope we have presented the facts of our accounts accurately. And lastly, we try not to be *too* opinionated, believe it or not.

We realize we may well have failed to mention someone's favourite place, be it Horsefly, Applegrove, Dog Creek, or some other of the hundreds of dots on the map of British Columbia. A community may be only a tiny dot on the map, but that doesn't mean it is of little consequence. Every town and village, past or present, has a special meaning to those for whom it was or is called "home." All we can say is that we had to save something for yet another book!

We do hope you enjoy reading *British Columbia 100 Years Ago* as much as we have enjoyed researching and presenting the pictures and stories.

Fred Thirkell   Bob Scullion

Fred Thirkell and Bob Scullion

INTRODUCTION

British Columbia Then and Now

The pictures following this introduction, and the stories they tell, have been grouped to represent nine different regions of the province.

Victoria and the Island, Vancouver and the Valley

The two regions in the southwest corner of the province have experienced considerable change over the last century. Victoria had its beginning in the 1840s when the Hudson's Bay Company established a fort on the southern tip of Vancouver Island in order to protect the interests of British fur traders. In 1858 it became the colonial capital of Vancouver Island, in 1866 the capital of the colony of British Columbia, and then in 1871 the provincial capital. It was not only a centre of government, but of trade, industry, and society as well. There were small pockets of agriculture, particularly on the Saanich Peninsula and in the Comox valley, logging around Chemainus, and seal and whale hunting, as well as fishing, off the Island's coast. But coal mining was the Island's chief industry a century ago. While coal was shipped from both Union Bay and Nanaimo, the Esquimalt & Nanaimo Railroad funnelled most of the Island's trade through Victoria. Even though Victoria still saw itself as the province's most important commercial centre in 1900, its status was changing, thanks to the CPR.

Before the the railway was completed to tidewater in 1887, British Columbia was little more than an isolated colonial territory, 14,000 miles from Great Britain by sea. After the CPR reached the west coast, the province was only 2,500 miles by rail from central Canada, and from there it was a relatively short Atlantic crossing to the markets of the mother country and Europe. By 1900, Vancouver, with a population of 30,000, had become the largest city in the province. Perhaps more importantly, Vancouver had captured not only the deep-sea trade, but also the mainland and North Coast trade.

Early Vancouver was an important port, as well as a city of sawmills and lumber yards. By 1910 there were some 25 mills and wood-product plants ringing False Creek.

Salmon canneries were concentrated along the banks of the Fraser River from Steveston to New Westminster. The Royal City, as New Westminster is known, had a population of approximately 6,300 in 1900 and was the market town for the Fraser Valley communities south of the river. Valley people, who for the most part had to travel to market over very bad roads or sail downriver by sternwheeler, were pleased when in 1904 the New Westminster bridge across the Fraser opened. They were even more pleased in 1910 when the B.C. Electric Railway completed its interurban line to Chilliwack. The trams, as they were more often called, created a fast and direct link to Vancouver via New Westminster. On Vancouver Island, the B.C. Electric had built a similar interurban line that ran from Victoria through the farmlands of the Saanich Peninsula. It did not succeed as did the Fraser Valley line and was abandoned in 1924.

This is not to say that Victoria and the Island were stagnating. Thanks in large part to the CPR, tourism became one of Victoria's prime industries. In 1901 the CPR bought out the Pacific Navigation Company and went on to build a fleet of luxury vessels, beginning with the *Princess Victoria*. In 1908 it opened the Empress Hotel, and Victoria's place as a premier tourist destination was assured.

So that's how it was "back then." What about now? Today the two regions go their separate and very different ways. Victoria is home to the provincial bureaucracy, the naval and coast guard establishments, and to many people who, in their retirement, have sought refuge from winter's fury. And, of course, as its citizens will tell you, Victoria is our nation's tourism capital, a title it both deserves and fights jealously to preserve. Up-Island things are a bit different. As the 21st century begins, forestry is the major industry and employer. Even though it has taken quite a beating from American duties and a depressed world market, it is still the industry that puts the food on many up-Island tables. Interestingly, places like Parksville, Qualicum, Comox, and Courtenay have in recent years attracted a fair number of retiring mainlanders.

Vancouver over the past century has become a mega multiethnic, multicultural city, swallowing up its neighbours—places like New Westminster, Steveston, Langley, Coquitlam, Port Moody, and Maple Ridge—and turning them into constituent parts of Greater Vancouver. While Victoria has firmly established its identity as the seat of government, a great place to retire, and a tourist mecca, Vancouver is still trying to legitimize its claim to being a "world-class" city, whatever that might be.

The Similkameen, The Boundary Country, and The West and East Kootenays

At the beginning of the 20th century, when the mineral wealth of the Canadian Shield was still largely unknown, British Columbia was considered the country's leading mineral-producing province. In the 1890s mineral deposits in what we call the Borderlands—that is, the Similkameen, the Boundary Country, and the West and East Kootenays—brought the first influx of settlers to the region. The Borderlands extend from around Princeton in the west to the Crowsnest Pass in the east, and from the international boundary in the south to an area 10 to 70 miles north.

The search for gold, copper, silver, lead, zinc, and coal brought new Borderland towns into existence almost overnight. It also jump-started the development of a rail and water-borne transportation system that saw fierce competition between the Canadian Pacific and Great Northern railroads. Naturally enough, it was gold above all else that was sought by the prospectors and miners, most of whom were Americans crossing into B.C. from neighbouring states. In 1899 gold was discovered at Hedley in the Similkameen; between 1901 and 1916 at Rossland in the West Kootenay, local mines produced half the gold mined in B.C.

Although silver was mined successfully from 1893 until 1929 at Moyie in the East Kootenay, it was in the part of the West Kootenay known as the Silvery Slocan that silver was king. The heyday of the many towns found between New Denver and Kaslo—places like Sandon, Three Forks, and Cody, which are ghost towns today—was between 1890 and 1914.

The Boundary Country, which stretches from Rock Creek in the west to Grand Forks in the east, was famed for its copper deposits and smelters a century ago. In 1903 Granby Consolidated blew in a smelter at Grand Forks to refine copper ore brought from the mines at Phoenix. It was the largest copper smelter in the British Empire prior to its closing in 1919. In 1901 the B.C. Copper Company smelter at Anaconda near Greenwood came into production. Like the smelter at Grand Forks and the much smaller one at Boundary Falls, it could not survive the drop in world copper prices that followed the Great War.

The most significant and lasting monument to mining in the Borderlands is the smelter at Trail. It went into production in 1896, and two years later it came into the hands of the CPR as part of a package deal involving local rail lines. In 1906 the CPR and others merged a number of mining interests, railways, and a light and power company to form the Consolidated Mining and Smelting Company (Cominco). The new company went on in 1910 to purchase Kimberley's Sullivan Mine, which would become the world's largest producer of lead and zinc.

The Sullivan Mine was in the East Kootenay, where the real wealth of the region was produced by black gold—that is, coal. In the 1890s significant anthracite deposits were found in the Elk River valley, and a number of mining towns—Fernie with its rows of coke ovens being the most significant—came into being.

While the Borderlands were not noted for agriculture, there were attempts at farming in the valleys. Fruit ranching held a special appeal in the early 1900s. Without doubt the most successful farms and fruit ranches were those in the Similkameen, around Keremeos. In the Boundary Country, particularly around Rock Creek and Midway, land agents worked hard in the years before the First World War to promote the area as potential orchard land. As it turned out, the cost of irrigation was such that would-be orchardists could not afford to turn the region into a second Okanagan. More successful at farming in both the Boundary Country and the West Kootenay were the Doukhobors, members of a Russian Christian sect who came to Canada seeking religious freedom. Some 5,000 ended up in B.C., with settlements near Grand Forks and Castlegar. Their lifestyle was initially communal, and while they were very good farmers, they lost most of their lands to creditors during the Depression. In the East Kootenay, at the south end of Kootenay Lake near Creston, a successful program of land reclamation created the only significant grain-growing area in the province outside the Peace River Block.

And what of today? To date the Borderlands have never been what they were in the years before the First World War. This isn't to say that nothing of importance has happened in the Southern Interior since 1918. While mining is no longer the region's chief industry—that distinction now belongs to forestry—minerals are still important money-makers. In the last quarter of the 20th century, strip mining profitably reworked the site of the old copper mines in Phoenix, and the tailings at Hedley have been reworked. The Elk River valley coalfield in the East Kootenay has also been strip-mined. As the century ended, B.C.'s coal exports produced revenue in excess of $1 billion annually.

Doubtless the region's most enduring symbol of success is Cominco's smelter at Trail. It is the world's largest zinc producer, and its product had a value of $231 million in 1998.

In the latter years of the last century, tourism became important, particularly in the Kootenays. History buffs love the ghost towns and the relatively unspoiled cities and towns, like Nelson and Kaslo. As well, the opportunities for winter sports have not been lost on the athletically inclined. Each year brings new visitors to the Borderlands, as well as new residents. Some are retired and have chosen a quieter (and more affordable) lifestyle, while others are seeking a less hectic and more positive environment in which to live and raise their families. As an example of beauty and industry living in harmony, the Borderlands have perhaps given a special gift to all British Columbians.

Through the Rockies and the Selkirks

By 1900, there was no longer any doubt that the CPR had successfully overcome the financial uncertainties that surrounded its birth. The fact that it was Canada's only transcontinental railway for the first 30 years of its existence almost guaranteed its success. Not that its managers counted on that alone for success. Early on, they took full advantage of the spectacular mountain scenery through which the line passed, and tourists, particularly wealthy ones, were actively courted. Sir William Van Horne, the company's president, would not settle for the Pullman sleeping cars that American railways leased, choosing instead to have CPR's passenger cars custom built to a higher standard of comfort, beauty, and safety. Unfortunately, it was not until the incredibly steep grade west of Field had been overcome by the creation of the Spiral Tunnels in 1909 that equally opulent (and much heavier) dining cars, in which a veritable sea of silver and fine glass was set before each diner, could be put into service in mountainous B.C.

Until then, as passengers had to eat, mountains or no mountains, Van Horne overcame the problem by building three hotels in the mountains that could also serve as all-important meal stops. They were at Field in the Rockies, Glacier in the Purcells, and at North Bend in the Fraser Canyon. Interestingly, until the Connaught Tunnel was put through in 1916, thereby rerouting the line away from Glacier House, the hotel was as popular, if not more so, than the Banff Springs Hotel in Alberta, particularly with mountaineers. Later, hotels were also opened at Revelstoke and Sicamous. They were built not only to attract tourists, but also to accommodate those who would be changing trains to travel down the Arrow Lakes or Okanagan Lake.

Today, railroading in the mountains is very different than it was 100 years ago. Spindly wooden bridges—built out of economic necessity—have been replaced by huge concrete-and-steel structures, and the rail weight has more than doubled to bear the vastly increased tonnage of modern trains, which are monitored and guided by radio from centralized traffic-control centres rather than by old-fashioned telegraph and manually operated signals.

Probably the greatest single change affecting train travel through the mountains has been the conversion from steam to diesel electric power. This change has revolutionized the movement of freight. A century ago, the length and weight of a train was determined by the limited traction steam engines could muster. The diesel electric locomotives, any number of which can be operated in tandem, are able to move trains over a mile in length through the mountains with little apparent effort. One topic discussed in 1895, and at least every 10 to 15 years since, is the electrification of the 480-mile-long main line from Calgary to Vancouver.

But whether powered by steam or diesel, the passenger train had all but disappeared in the course of the 20th century. The creation of new highways, which often follow old railway right-of-ways, and safe efficient airlines have made the train an "also-ran" option for most of the travelling public. In 1978 a fully integrated CP/CN passenger service known as VIA Rail came into being. A Crown corporation, VIA Rail is responsible for the country's passenger rail service. While the corporation has created corridor services around principal cities in central Canada, in B.C. passenger service has been reduced to one train a day in and out of Vancouver, at fares most people can't afford.

In terms of size, the towns along the line—places like Field, Golden, and Revelstoke—remain much as they were 100 years ago. The people in these towns and others like them are thankful, of course, that so many people still want to travel through the mountains and stop to enjoy the hospitality they provide.

The Thompson-Okanagan

A century ago, both the Thompson and the Okanagan grasslands were given over primarily to cattle ranching. True, there was some dairy farming and a few apple orchards between Sicamous and Vernon, but it was cattle ranching that attracted the region's original White settlers. It wasn't long, however, before things began to change.

Kamloops, located as it is at the confluence of the North and South Thompson rivers, has been at the heart of the Southern Interior almost from the day it came into being as a fur-trading post in 1912. Later in the 19th century, particularly after the arrival of the CPR, the town became the supply and service centre for the mines, ranches, and farms of the Dry Belt. Its importance was further enhanced when, early in the 20th century, the CNR also came through the town, heading, like the CPR before it, down the Thompson-Fraser river system to Vancouver. Kamloops gained still greater importance as a commercial, distribution, transportation, and service centre when it became the junction of the Trans-Canada and Yellowhead highways. Today forestry and mining are more important in dollar value to the city and region's economy than is ranching. With a population of more than 76,000, Kamloops is very much the Dry Belt's subregional capital.

In the Okanagan at the beginning of the 20th century, considerable effort went into attracting settlers "of the right sort" to the region. In their *British Columbia*, Boam and Brown wrote: "There are few places that offer greater attractions to the man of comparatively small means who wishes to break away from the stress of business or professional life in the great cities than the Okanagan Valley." Boam and Brown also said at the time that "most of the farms [are] from 10 to 20 acres, which is quite sufficient to yield a comfortable income to the owners, many of whom are retired army and navy officers, ex-lawyers, doctors and civil servants who unite in making social life as pleasant as that obtaining in English country districts."

It was not until after the First World War that serious fruit farming, dependent as it was on irrigation, really came into its own. Apples grew well in the northern half of the 250-mile-long valley and found a ready market in the Prairies and in Europe. Soft fruits like peaches, cherries, and pears, which did well around Summerland, Penticton, and Osoyoos where the climate was both hotter and dryer, sold well on the coast and on the Prairies. The completion of the CPR's Kettle Valley Railroad in 1916 opened new markets to southern Okanagan growers and to the fruit-processing plants of Penticton.

The Okanagan has experienced phenomenal change in the latter part of the 20th century. Who could have imagined a mere 50 years ago that the cultivation of grapes and the production of fine wines would become such an important part of the Okanagan's life and economy? While the lake has been a favourite summer sunspot for a great many years, particularly for Albertans, the Coquihalla Highway has placed the Okanagan within easy driving distance for those living on the coast and the region has done much to make its luxury resorts and fashionable wineries into a winning combination for those looking for something different but not too far from home.

Northern British Columbia and the North Coast

One hundred years ago, northern British Columbia was still largely the undisputed territory of First Nations people. The only non-Natives in the region were hunters and trappers, Hudson's Bay Company employees working in trading posts at places like Hazleton, and prospectors seeking their Eldorado in the north.

On the North Coast, there were non-Native populations in small centres like Port Essington and Port Simpson. These communities had come into being in the 19th century to take advantage of the rich harvest to be taken from the sea.

Between 1907 and 1914 the Grand Trunk Pacific Railway's main line from Edmonton was built through the upper Fraser, Bulkley and Skeena valleys on its way to the Pacific. While small towns came into being in the Bulkley and Nechako valleys, and the port of Prince Rupert was created on Kaien Island, the line attracted very little business. As fate would have it, the depression of 1912-13 and the Great War of 1914-18 forced the railway company into bankruptcy. None of the settlements along the rail line experienced any significant growth between the two world wars.

In contrast, the years before the First World War were a time of relative prosperity on the North Coast. There were many small fishing communities along the coast and 90 or more salmon canneries in the estuaries of the Skeena and Naas rivers. In the course of the century the situation changed radically: by the 1950s the number of canneries was down to 30; by the year 2000 only eight large canneries were still in operation. Today, only 40 percent of the salmon caught is canned, and the rest is either frozen, smoked, salted, or marketed fresh.

Although lumbering has always been important in the north—Prince George had 16 sawmills in operation soon after being founded in 1909 —it really didn't take off until after the Second World War. By the end of the 20th century, logging operations and sawmills were major employers in Quesnel, Burns

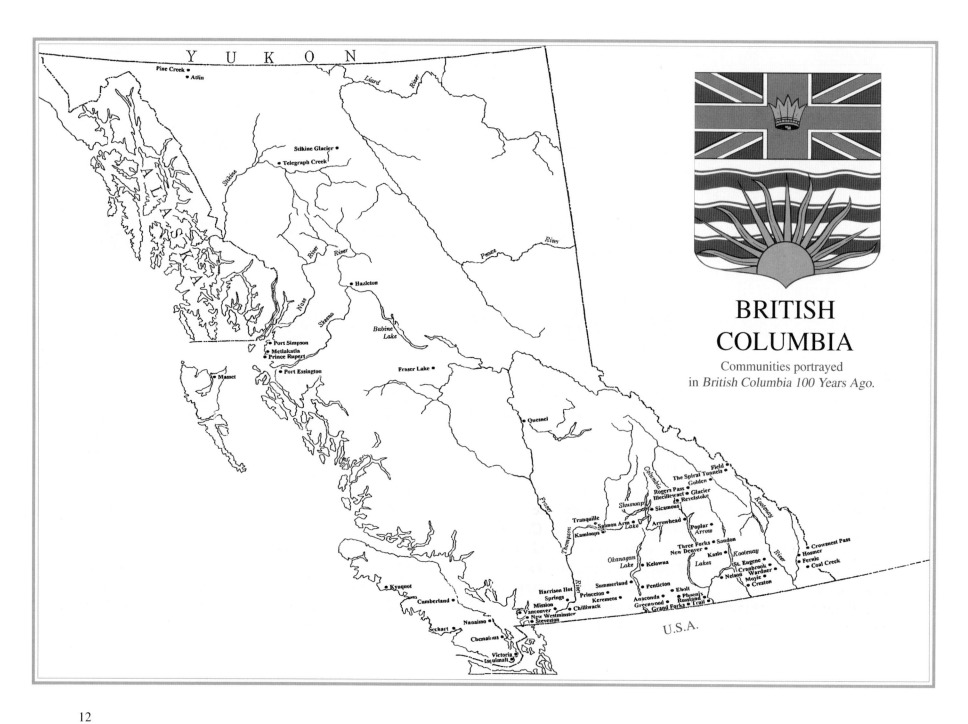

BRITISH COLUMBIA

Communities portrayed
in *British Columbia 100 Years Ago.*

YUKON

Pine Creek •
• Atlin

Liard *River*

Stikine Glacier •
• Telegraph Creek

ALASKA

Stikine

River
River

Nass

Peace *River*

• Hazleton

Skeena

Babine Lake

Port Simpson •
• Metlakatla
• Prince Rupert

Fraser Lake •

• Masset

• Port Essington

• Quesnel

Fraser

Columbia

Field •
The Spiral Tunnels •
Golden •
Rogers Pass •
Illecillewaet • • Glacier
• Revelstoke

Shuswap
Lake
• Sicamous
Tranquille •
Salmon Arm •
• Arrowhead
Poplar •
Arrow
Kamloops •

Thompson

Kootenay

Three Forks • • Sandon
New Denver •
• Kaslo
Kootenay
Lakes
• St. Eugene
• Cranbrook
Nelson • • Wardner
• Moyie
• Creston

• Crowsnest Pass
• Hosmer
• Fernie
• Coal Creek

Okanagan
Lake
• Kelowna

River

• Kyuquot

Harrison Hot
Springs •
Princeton •
Keremeos •
Summerland •
• Penticton
Anaconda •
Greenwood •
• Eholt
• Phoenix
Rossland •

Cumberland •

Mission •
• Vancouver
• New Westminster
• Steveston
Chilliwack •
Grand Forks • • Trail

River

U.S.A.

Sechart •
Nanaimo •
Chemainus •
Victoria •
Esquimalt •

Lake, Smithers, Hazleton, and Terrace. While of less importance than agriculture, mining, and gas and oil exploration and production, forestry is nevertheless a significant money-maker in Dawson Creek, Fort St. John, and other communities in the far north of the province.

Another change from "back then" to "now" relates to the development of hydroelectric power. Energy from the Peace River has not only provided power for industry in Prince George, a city of 75,000, but for the aluminum smelter at Kitimat as well.

Such mines as existed in northern B.C. 100 years ago were in the province's mountainous northwestern corner near Atlin. Not too far away, an asbestos mine opened at Cassiar in 1952 and was in production until 1991. Generally speaking, in the part of B.C. that lies behind the Alaska Panhandle mines of one sort or another have been in operation throughout much of the last century.

What of tourism in northern B.C.? It is probably safe to say that at least 10 times as many British Columbians have been to California and Disneyland as have been to "central" B.C. cities like Prince George and Prince Rupert, let alone truly northern communities like Fort Nelson, Stewart, and Atlin. But thanks to B.C. Rail, B.C. Ferries, air travel, and highways that have been created and/or vastly improved over the past century, more and more people are visiting northern B.C. and the North Coast for the first time. Certainly there were always a few people visiting the north, particularly in big-game season! The tourists today, though, are for the most part very different from those who went north even a quarter-century ago. Whether they know it or not, they are eco-tourists—that is, people who have come to enjoy the natural wonders and beauty of the region without plundering. Through heightened awareness, this new breed of tourist exhibits a changed perceptive. As they travel, they may still regard the largely unoccupied northern vastness as empty land, but they no longer see it as useless land.

Thinking not only of northern British Columbia and the North Coast but of the whole province, it is important for all British Columbians to remember that their provincial motto, *splendor sine occasu* ("splendour without diminishment"), can only have real meaning if they, through their attitudes and actions, give it meaning.

The reference map (opposite page).

Many of the communities that thrived a century ago are little known in our generation. In the interest of featuring these locations and providing geopgraphic perspective, only locations highlighted in this book have beeen identified on the map.

VICTORIA—THE EMPRESS HOTEL

It would be safe to say that the average tourist sees two buildings as defining Victoria: one is the Legislature and the other is the Empress Hotel. Though very different in style, both were designed by Francis Rattenbury. The plans for the Empress began as a reworking of an earlier design for a CPR hotel in the Chateau style to be built in Vancouver. The second Hotel Vancouver was ultimately built in a Renaissance Revival style, and Victoria ended up with a hotel in the highly successful CPR Chateau style.

The original plans for the Empress Hotel called for construction in three phases. First the main block, as pictured, was to be built, and then north and south wings were to be added. The contract for the $465,000 main block was signed in May 1905, and the 165-room hotel opened on January 22, 1908. The north and south wings planned by Rattenbury were built between 1909 and 1914, under the supervision of another CPR architect, W. S. Painter. It was Painter who also added the ballroom in 1912 and a picturesque second wing to the hotel's north side in 1929.

Empress Hotel. Victoria, B. C.

15

VICTORIA—HATLEY PARK

Hatley Park was the home of James Dunsmuir, in his time one of the two most hated men in B.C., the other being his father, Robert. The latter owned the coal mines at Wellington and headed the syndicate that received a land grant equal to 20 percent of Vancouver Island to build the Esquimalt & Nanaimo Railroad. James became as infamous as his father for his inhumane treatment of his miners and tenants.

James Dunsmuir's home would have satisfied any robber baron of his day. Sited on a 650-acre waterfront property, it was designed by Samuel Maclure, B.C.'s leading society architect. The castle had everything—fine stonework, magnificent stained glass, staircases crafted in Chicago, an immense fourth-floor ballroom, and seemingly endless other rooms decorated in the Arts and Crafts style. The estate remained in the family until 1940, when it was sold to the federal government for $75,000 initially to become Royal Roads, Canada's naval college.

NEW DUNSMUIR CASTLE, HATLEY PARK, VICTORIA B. C.

ESQUIMALT—A "MUST-SEE" VILLAGE

Fort Victoria was established in 1843, and by the 1850s much of nearby Esquimalt had been cleared and developed as farmland. It remained bucolic for some time. In 1889, one Maturin Ballou wrote that while "a macadamized road connects Esquimalt with Victoria [it runs] between fragrant hedges, past charming cottages and through delightful pine groves." Esquimalt was also described as a "must-see" village for visitors. But it was more than a quaint outpost.

A military garrison had been stationed at Work Point Barracks in 1887, and the village was also home to a Dominion Meteorological Station. With the opening of the Esquimalt Marine Railway in 1898, shipbuilding became an important local industry. The introduction of regular service on the Esquimalt & Nanaimo Railway in the same year gave the community a further boost. Streetcars, introduced in 1890, made Esquimalt a practical residential possibility for town folk wanting to escape the hubbub of the big city! Esquimalt was also home to a naval dockyard, but that's another story.

Esquimalt.

ESQUIMALT—THE ROYAL NAVY

The Royal Navy arrived on the North Pacific coast in 1846, the year in which the Treaty of Washington was signed. Although the treaty settled the Oregon boundary dispute, the navy was to contain further American ambitions in the region. In 1855, Governor Douglas allocated money for a naval hospital to be opened at Esquimalt. Given that Alaska was still Russian territory, it was remotely possible that the Crimean War of 1854-55 might spill over into the Pacific. In 1865, Esquimalt became home to the Royal Navy's Pacific Squadron, replacing Valparaiso, Chile, where it had been stationed since 1837. The Dockyard at Esquimalt had a dry dock 450 feet long, 65 feet wide, and 26 feet deep that could accommodate the largest British warship in the Pacific.

As the 20th century opened, Britain was looking for ways to reduce the cost of maintaining its fleet, and by 1902 had decided to decommission its Canadian naval bases at Halifax and Esquimalt. In 1910, the naval establishments were transferred to Canada when the Naval Service Act that brought the Royal Canadian Navy into being was passed.

H.M.S. Flora in Esquimalt Dry Dock, near Victoria, B. C.

CHEMAINUS—MR. HUMBIRD'S MILL

It is sometimes assumed that American involvement in British Columbia's forest industry is a recent phenomenon. Such is not the case. By the 1890s many of the province's logging operations and sawmills were controlled by men like A. Humbird, a Wisconsin sawmill operator who had founded the Victoria Lumber and Manufacturing Company in 1889. Beginning with a stand of timber and a mill at Chemainus bought from the Dunsmuirs, he soon owned one of the largest lumber operations in B.C.

The Victoria Lumber and Manufacturing Company was one of the first in the province to build a logging railway. It went into operation in 1900 with a 45-ton, gear-driven Climax locomotive and was a great success. Whereas only 110 loggers were employed before the railway was put through to the timberlands, once it was in operation 225 men were needed to work in the woods, and of course, they increased production.

Logging at Chemainus, Vancouver Island, B.C.

NANAIMO—AN EARLY COAL TOWN

In 1851, the Hudson's Bay Company was made aware of coal deposits at Nanaimo. In the following year, James Douglas went to have a look at the coal beds for himself. Upon his return to Victoria he sent Joseph Mackay to take formal possession of the deposits for the company. Before long a small mining community came into being, and on September 10, 1852, coal was first shipped from Nanaimo.

While the local Natives were peaceable and friendly, tribes from farther north were not: their raiding parties could arrive at any time. In 1853, for protection and safety, a bastion or blockhouse was built. It was 30 feet high and had three floors. On the first were the Hudson's Bay Company office and stores, on the second were an arsenal and cannons, and on the top floor there was space for the town's inhabitants should the settlement be attacked. The mines were sold to the Vancouver Coal Mining and Land Company in 1862 and continued to produce until the 1950s.

Bastion Street — Nanaimo

CUMBERLAND—CANADA'S SMALLEST CITY

In 1893 James Dunsmuir created a townsite to the east of his Union Colliery. He named it Cumberland in honour of the English county so well known for its coal mines. When incorporated as a city in 1897, Cumberland's claim to fame was that it became at once both the smallest and most westerly city in North America. By 1900, one-quarter of its population were Asians brought from other Dunsmuir mines and from China to work in the pits at Cumberland.

In keeping with the city's name, many streets like Windermere, Derwent, Keswick, and Penrith are English Lake District names. Cumberland's Penrith Avenue was an avenue of churches. By 1895, there were Anglican, Roman Catholic, Presbyterian, and Methodist congregations. Cumberland also had a Presbyterian Chinese Mission and a Methodist Japanese Mission. A declining population and mine closures forced Cumberland to revert to village status in 1958. Such are the vicissitudes of time.

Penrith Avenue, Cumberland, British Columbia. Published by T. N. Hibben & Co., Victoria, British Columbia. No. 121

KYUQUOT—AN INDIAN BURIAL GROUND

The Kyuquot people are part of the Nuu-chah-nulth (Nootka) First Nation. Their lands are at the northern limits of the traditional Nootka territories, on the west coast of Vancouver Island. It was not until the 1850s that White traders visited Kyuquot Sound regularly, and then it was to barter for fish oil.

The Kyuquot recognized certain supernatural forces, as did all the Nuu-chah-nulth people, which they believed could be controlled by ritual and ceremony. Not surprisingly, death and the dead were feared, and the handling of a corpse was taken most seriously. Bodies of chiefs and the wealthy were flexed—that is, folded—into boxes or canoes that were placed in trees, caves, or on points of land. The bodies of poorer folk were buried in mats or older blankets in shallow graves. Valuables were often deposited with the dead. Rightly or wrongly, many Native artifacts found today in both public and private collections came from such burial sites.

Indian Burial Ground, Kyuquot, B. C.

SECHART—WHALING

Commercial whaling began on the west coast of British North America in 1834 when Yankee whalers rounded Cape Horn to hunt off the northwest coast. No locally based whaling companies came on the scene until the beginning of the 20th century. By then, hunting with harpoons thrown from longboats was a thing of the past; the new harpoon guns, carrying a dynamite charge that exploded on impact, instantly killed the whales.

In 1908, Victoria's Pacific Whaling Company, with one of its five plants at Sechart in Barkley Sound, processed over 500 whales at its stations. Whale oil was shipped to Glasgow, bone fertilizer went to Hawaii, and salted whale meat was transported in barrels to Japan.

In some years, Pacific Whaling paid its shareholders dividends of 25 percent. By the 1950s, however, changing attitudes had made whaling, like seal hunting before it, a closed chapter in British Columbia's fishing history.

PHOTO BY ARTHUR W. McCURDY.   A WHALING STATION, VANCOUVER ISLAND.

THE GULF OF GEORGIA—THE *PRINCESS VICTORIA*

I n 1901, the CPR bought Canadian Pacific Navigation for $5.31 million. Of the 14 ships acquired, almost all had been pre-owned. The CPR was soon aware of the need for new and faster vessels for its coastal service. In 1902, the hull was assembled and the engines installed in the new *Princess Victoria* at Newcastle-upon-Tyne, but because a British shipyards strike was expected, the magnificent ship's superstructure was not completed until the vessel reached Vancouver.

The *Princess Victoria*'s speed and luxury meant that the Edwardian tourist was indeed travelling in high style. Its cruising speed of 19.5 knots made the vessel the fastest on the coast and able to maintain a seemingly impossible schedule. The ship left Victoria for Vancouver at 7:30 a.m. and returned to Victoria at 1:00 p.m. It then left for Seattle at 7:00 p.m., returning to Victoria at midnight, having sailed 327 miles in a day.

PRINCESS VICTORIA.

PRINCESS VICTORIA

VANCOUVER—HASTINGS MILL

Hastings Mill first came into being as Stamp's Mill in June 1865. It did not actually get into production until 1867 when its machinery finally arrived from Glasgow, Scotland. Even at that, it was the first mill to be built on the south shore of Burrard Inlet. In 1859, the irascible Captain Stamp fell out with his British backers and the mill was sold to Heatley & Co. of London, who appointed J. A. Raymur manager. John Hendry bought the mill in 1889, merging it with his Royal City Planing Mills to form B.C. Mills, Timber and Trading Company.

Hastings Mill's site encompassed 20 acres along 2,080 feet of Burrard Inlet. In 1911, the mill produced 125 million board feet of lumber. It is interesting to note that by then, B.C. Mills, Timber and Trading was using a fleet of seven steamships for lumber shipments. The small fleet of foreign-owned square-rigged sailing ships loading at Hastings Mill suggests that the firm was considerably ahead of its time.

Vessel Loading Lumber, Vancouver, B. C.

VANCOUVER—THE CPR STATION

By 1890, the CPR realized that its original wooden station was inadequate for the needs of the fast-growing city of Vancouver. A magnificent new $200,000 station in the Chateau style was to be built at the foot of Granville Street. The architect chosen to design the building was Edward Maxwell, one of the country's finest, who had already designed a number of stations and hotels for the CPR.

Like most of Maxwell's other buildings, the station was essentially a Georgian neo-classical structure dressed in High Victorian picturesque detailing. Perhaps its most impressive feature was the 42-foot arched entrance that was faced in rusticated Calgary limestone. While its foundations were in place in 1892, the CPR delayed further construction until 1897. Unfortunately, when the building opened in 1899, it was already unable to handle the volume of rail traffic moving in and out of Vancouver. Sadly, this very fine building had to be razed to make room for the third station, built between 1907 and 1914, that now serves as the city's SeaBus and SkyTrain terminal.

Vancouver B. C.   Canadian Pacific Railway Station

Illustrated Post Card Co, Montreal.

VANCOUVER—HOTEL VANCOUVER

It is difficult to write about Vancouver without mentioning the CPR, which gave the city its shape and importance. Even its original Hotel Vancouver at Granville and Georgia helped determine the direction in which the city would grow. Built in a simplified Chateau style, it opened on May 16, 1887. While it was comfortable enough, it wasn't much to look at. Its architect, Thomas Sorby, who knew the railway's penny-pinching ways only too well, described it as "a building without architecture."

In 1901, Francis Rattenbury was called in to prepare plans for an entirely new Italian Renaissance hotel, of which only one small piece was ever built. The CPR had decided not to proceed with the project, and nothing further was done until 1912-1916, when a new hotel was finally built on the old site. Its architect, Francis Swales, incorporated Rattenbury's Howe Street building into his new design.

HOTEL VANCOUVER.

1557.

STEVESTON—WHERE SALMON WAS KING

In 1911, the B.C. Year Book reported that most of the fish used for canning were sockeye salmon, and that "as many as 2,000 boats [each with a two-man crew] are seen at the mouth of the Fraser River at one time, and in big runs they will average from 100 to 500 fish each night." The industry began in 1876 with a pack of about 10,000 cases, and by 1897 over one million cases with a value of $4.9 million were shipped abroad. In that each case of salmon weighed 48 pounds, it meant that 48 million pounds of salmon were being shipped overseas in one season. The average 1897 income of a White fisherman was $600; Natives and Japanese made less.

When a tug with its scow full of salmon arrived from the fishing grounds, it was time for the men and women in the canneries to go to work. And in 1897 going to work could mean putting in 10- to 16-hour days. While Chinese were paid more, Native women only got 15 to 20 cents an hour.

Salmon from the traps.

NEW WESTMINSTER—COLUMBIA STREET

Columbia Street has a newish look about it because an 1898 fire destroyed much of the old business district and public buildings. The tall, unfinished building on the left of the postcard was Westminster Trust Company's new head office.

The stone-trimmed brick building on the southeast corner of Columbia and Eighth streets was the B.C. Electric's 1911 interurban station. At street level, the new $80,000 station had three tracks running through the building, a general waiting room, a ladies' waiting room, and ticket offices. Maintaining order on the ground floor and on the platform was a special constable who also announced the trains. One floor up were 21 offices, four bedrooms for emergency crews, and a classroom for instructing motormen and conductors. The building's foundations were such that additional floors could be added as needed. None, however, were ever needed.

New Westminster's streetcars were replaced by buses in 1937. On July 31, 1954, the interurban depot closed for the last time, and trams became the stuff of which memories are made.

Columbia Street, New Westminster, B.C.

NEW WESTMINSTER—THE NEW BRIDGE

The first bridge built across the lower reaches of the Fraser River was the $1-million bridge at New Westminster. It was opened July 23, 1904, and events on the big day included Native canoe races, a procession of steamers, a civic luncheon, a torchlight procession on the river, and fireworks sent heavenward from the bridge's upper deck.

It would be difficult to overestimate the importance of the new bridge. The train tracks on the bridge's lower level allowed the Great Northern Railway to enter Vancouver and gave the B.C. Electric Railway access to the Fraser Valley. As well, the Canadian Northern (later the CNR) was also to come into Vancouver via the new bridge. The upper deck accommodated wagons and motor vehicles and was a great boon to Fraser Valley farmers for whom New Westminster was an important market town.

After the Pattullo Bridge opened in 1937, the old bridge was closed to motor traffic, and its upper deck was removed. The structure is still used as a train bridge, and the CNR, which owns it, has spent over $15 million on upgrades.

NEW GOVERNMENT BRIDGE OVER FRASER RIVER FOR PASSENGER AND RAILROAD TRAFFIC - NEW WESTMINSTER, B.C.

PUBL. BY NORMAN CAPLE & CO. VANCOUVER B.C.

MISSION—ONCE AN IMPORTANT JUNCTION

Mission is 40 miles east of Vancouver on the main line of the CPR. It had its beginning in the 1860s when the Oblates of Mary Immaculate established a residential school for Native children. In 1899, the CPR opened a branch line crossing the Fraser from Mission to Huntington on the U.S. border to provide an interchange with American railroads.

Until the bridge at New Westminster opened in 1904, the Mission–Huntington interchange was the only direct rail connection to the United States. While 16 passenger trains and innumerable freights trains passed *through* Mission every day, they did the town little good. It was not until 1903, when the CPR introduced the "Agassiz Local," running from Ruby Creek to Vancouver in the morning and returning in the evening, that the railway had any real impact on life in Mission. The local could be flagged down anywhere along its route and was particularly popular on Saturday—Market Day—when people made their way to Mission to sell produce, shop, socialize, and take a break from a life that could be both hard and monotonous.

Transcontinental Train at Mission Jct. B. C.

CHILLIWACK—AN OLD VALLEY TOWN

Chilliwack is on the south side of the Fraser River, 48 miles east of New Westminster. The township was incorporated in 1873, and a village soon developed within it at a crossroads known as Five Corners. Named Centreville in 1883, the community was incorporated as the city of Chilliwack in 1908. A century ago transportation was a real problem for the people of Chilliwack. They had to make their way to New Westminster by way of the Old Yale Road, or take the sternwheeler downriver, or cross the Fraser and board a CPR train at Harrison River Station. All of that changed on October 3, 1910, when the B.C. Electric Company inaugurated interurban service between Vancouver and Chilliwack.

While shopping malls have changed the face of nearly every town in B.C., including Chilliwack, Five Corners is still thought of as the city's centre. Perhaps the biggest change in the look of Five Corners took place in 1909 when the Anglicans moved St. Thomas's Church from its rather restricted site to a larger property. The land was sold for $23,000; downtown real estate was expensive even in those days.

Westminster Street, Looking Toward Five Corners, Chilliwack, B.C.

HARRISON HOT SPRINGS—THE ST. ALICE HOTEL

The scene in front of the St. Alice Hotel at Harrison Hot Springs is one of Edwardian charm and propriety. The young men are seated on the grass near their bicycles, and the young women in straw hats, blouses, and skirts are seated in groups, which, while distant, are not *too* distant from their admirers. The picture suggests many possibilities.

Accommodating 130 guests, the hotel opened in 1886. It was a three-story L-shaped building with verandahs and balconies. On the ground floor was a dining room seating 75, a billiard room, gift shop, bar, reception area, and offices. The upper floors were given over to guest accommodation. The hotel was advertised as "a beautiful drive from Agassiz Station … with croquet lawns, tennis courts, fishing and boating." Prospective guests were also told that "the efficacy of the Harrison waters in rheumatism, kidney and liver diseases, etc. is well noted." The hotel, "Steam Heated and Electric Lighted throughout," charged $2.50 per day and upward, American Plan, with mineral baths, etc. extra. The St. Alice burned down in 1920, and the present-day Harrison Hotel opened in 1926.

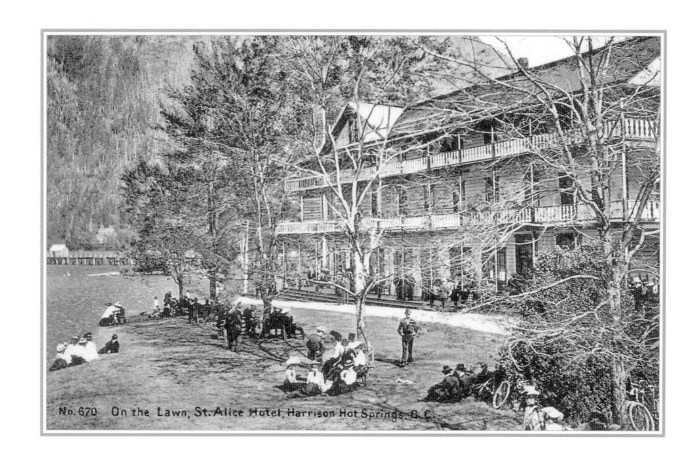

No. 670   On the Lawn, St. Alice Hotel, Harrison Hot Springs, B.C.

PRINCETON—ROYALLY NAMED

Princeton is located at the junction of the Similkameen and Tulameen rivers, 81 miles east of Hope and 40 miles west of Penticton. The town's pioneer settler was John Allison, who established a ranch at the confluence of the rivers in 1859. At the time, the area was known simply as Vermillion Forks, in reference to the colour of the banks of the Tulameen River. In 1860, Governor Douglas asked Allison to explore the Similkameen River valley. While doing this, Allison discovered the pass through the Cascades that bears his name.

Douglas had the townsite surveyed in 1860 and named Princeton in honour of Edward, Prince of Wales (later King Edward VII), who was visiting Canada at the time. In 1909, the Great Northern provided Princeton with its first rail connection to the outside world. A line was built from Oroville, Washington, through Keremeos to Princeton and on to Brookmere.

Near Princeton there were a number of mining communities, including Granite Creek, Copper Mountain, and Coalmont. At the beginning of the 20th century, Princeton was an important supply centre for these places and others like them.

Princeton B. C.

Totem Series No. 80.

Photo A. Murchie, Princeton, B. C.

53

KEREMEOS—EDEN ON THE SIMILKAMEEN

On the Similkameen River, Keremeos is an old established settlement 25 miles southwest of Penticton. From 1864 to 1872, it was the site of a Hudson's Bay trading post. Arriving in the mid-1860s, the community's first permanent settlers were cattle ranchers. By 1900, however, fruit farming had become the community's main industry. At that time Keremeos could be reached from the United States by one of the Great Northern's many branch lines that made their way into Canada or by stagecoaches that ran to and from Penticton three times a week.

A century ago Keremeos was an up-and-coming place, with land companies, a druggist, a hardware store, a branch of the Eastern Township Bank, and its very own newspaper, the *Keremeos Trumpet*. Pictured in its Dominion Day bunting is one of the town's more progressive businesses, G. G. Keeler's General Store and Restaurant. In the place of honour at the centre of the picture stands the vehicle that must have been G. G. Keeler's pride and joy: his truck, bearing the legend Keeler's Auto Transport. Keeler obviously meant business!

Keremeos, B. C.

GREENWOOD—COPPER STREET

During the boom years before the First World War, Greenwood's population soared to over 3,000. Situated in B.C.'s mineral-rich Boundary District, the city, which was incorporated in 1897, was first and foremost a mining town.

From 1901 until 1918, when the bottom suddenly dropped out of the copper market, Greenwood's chief employer was the B.C. Copper Company, with its head offices in New York City. Its smelter and concentrator at nearby Anaconda employed 450 men and on average produced 450,000 tons of copper per year. The ore came from three company-owned mines: Mother Lode, Wellington Camp, and Summit Camp.

Two miles long and half a mile wide, the town was typical of its day. It had four churches, five lodges, a public school, a brewery, two weekly newspapers, a hospital—St. Joseph of Peace—a telephone exchange, twelve hotels, and at least as many saloons as there were hotels. Perhaps not surprisingly, Greenwood's main avenue is Copper Street. The mines, as well as the smelter, have long since closed.

Copper Street, Greenwood, B.C.

ANACONDA—THE B.C. COPPER COMPANY

The Boundary District townsite of Anaconda was established in 1896. Located 12 miles east of Grand Forks and a mile south of Greenwood, it was the site of the B.C. Copper Company's smelter from 1901 until 1918. Much of the ore came from B.C. Copper's Mother Lode mine in Deadwood, which was three miles northwest of Greenwood. When in full production, the smelter's three blast furnaces were able to treat 2,600 tons of ore per day.

As the final part of the smelting process a small steam engine pushed four or five cone-shaped cars out to the slag heap where the molten residue was dumped. Each slagpot, as the rail cars were called, held 25 tons of slag. The smelter's chimney was built of a quarter-million bricks and stood 120 feet high. Its remains are the most significant reminder of the town's past glory. And rightly so, as the old smokestack was the tallest in the province.

Slag running into pots, each of 25 tons capacity, at B.C.
Copper Co's Smelter, Greenwood B.C.

EHOLT—GONE, AND ALMOST FORGOTTEN

Eholt came into being in the spring of 1898 when nearby deposits of copper, gold, and silver were discovered. At the top of the grade between Greenwood and Grand Forks, the new town became a divisional point on the CPR's Columbia and Western Railway. From Eholt, trains left the main line to travel the nine miles to Phoenix to bring copper ore back to Granby Consolidated's smelter in Grand Forks, 16 miles east of Eholt. Within the year, the CPR had laid out a townsite, built a station, engine house, coal tower, water tower, and installed a weigh scale.

By 1905, however, the town was already in decline. Local mines were not producing as it was hoped they would, and by 1908 people were moving away in significant numbers. As though things weren't bad enough, in August 1912 a fire destroyed the centre of town. Later in the same year the CPR moved its facilities to Grand Forks. The collapse in world copper prices in the 1920s left the town with fewer than 100 citizens. When the post office closed in 1947 there were only 17 people left in town. The last resident left Eholt in 1960.

C.P.R. Yards at Eholt, B.C. The railway centre of the Boundary.

PHOENIX—A TOWN LONG GONE

In the 1890s a mining town came into being at Phoenix, five miles east of Greenwood. The big name on the mountain was Granby Consolidated. The value of the copper deposits at Phoenix increased considerably when, in 1900, the CPR's branch line reached the community and the Granby Company's smelter at Grand Forks was blown in. In 1905, over 800 men were working in 50 miles of interconnected tunnels beneath the streets of Phoenix.

The price of copper dropped worldwide at the end of the First World War. Even though the company had extracted over $100 million worth of ore between 1900 and 1919, the party was over. In 1919, Granby Consolidated developed its holdings at Anyox on the northwest coast, abandoning Phoenix to the elements. After the Second World War Phoenix had a reprieve of sorts. The price of copper was such that open-pit mining became a practical option. Once the site had been worked over, however, the remains of the old town were no more. Ironically, the cemetery and its Great War memorial are the only signs of life left in Phoenix today.

Ironsides Mine, Phoenix, B. C.
On Line of Canadian Pacific Ry.

GRAND FORKS—GRANBY CONSOLIDATED

Incorporated as a city in 1897, Grand Forks was named for its location at the confluence of the Kettle and Granby rivers. The town came into its own in 1900, when Granby Consolidated chose it as the site for its new smelter. The town and the company had much for which to thank the CPR; the railway was at last able to guarantee a steady supply of smelting coal from the Crowsnest Pass fields and had completed its branch line from Eholt to the rich copper mines at Phoenix.

The smelter processed 2,000 tons of ore per day and employed 400 men. It is worth noting that, in 1905, Granby Consolidated introduced the eight-hour working day to Canada. By 1910, Grand Forks' copper smelter had become the world's second largest. It all came to an end in 1919, however, when postwar world copper prices took a plunge. The Granby company decided to consolidate its operations at Anyox on the North Coast, where it had equally rich yet more cheaply accessible copper deposits.

Granby Smelter — Grand Forks, B.C.

GRAND FORKS—THE COMPETITORS

The Canadian Pacific and Great Northern railways battled each other long and hard in British Columbia. Ironically, the CPR's chief executive was the American-born Sir William Van Horne, while the creator of the Great Northern was the Canadian-born James J. Hill. It was B.C.'s mineral wealth that legitimized their intense rivalry. The CPR's Crowsnest route ran along B.C.'s southern boundary, with branch lines heading off to wherever money could be made. By 1907, the GNR had crossed the border at ten different points and had over 300 miles of track in the Southern Interior.

The lines into Phoenix were typical of the rivalry. In 1901, the CPR completed its branch line from Eholt. The steep grade *averaged* 3.4 percent. Having had difficulty acquiring a right-of-way, the GNR's line between Grand Forks and Phoenix wasn't ready for business until 1905. But being second wasn't all that bad. Its grades were much easier than those of the CPR, and that meant the American line could make up longer trains and move them at greater speed. The Great Northern soon had the lion's share of the business.

C. P. R. O. & E. Train crossing The Granby Smelter Dam.

ARROWHEAD—LAKE STERNWHEELERS

It was the Columbia and Kootenay Steam Navigation Company that established the first scheduled steamship service on the Arrow Lakes. By the 1890s mining was attracting armies of men to the Kootenays and the company flourished. In 1897, the firm, whose sternwheelers sailed all the major interior routes, was bought out by the CPR for $200,000.

The *Trail* was built at Nakusp in 1896, primarily for freight service between Arrowhead and Trail. It burned in 1900. The *Rossland* was built at Nakusp in 1897 to provide an express passenger service on the Arrow Lakes. It provided a reliable service until 1917, when it was crushed by ice and sank at the wharf in Nakusp. The *Minto* was a prefab vessel, shipped by rail from Ontario in 1898 and assembled in Nakusp. It continued to sail the Arrow Lakes until passenger service was discontinued in 1954.

C.P.R. Strs. "Rossland," "Minto," and "Trail," at Arrowhead, Columbia River, B.C.

NEW DENVER—FOOTBALL A.K.A. SOCCER

Football was played throughout British Columbia long before it had to be renamed *soccer* to accommodate the Americans, who had appropriated the name for their totally different game that evolved out of *rugby football*. Football, or soccer, was introduced to mainland B.C. by the Royal Engineers stationed in New Westminster. The first documented game took place at Queens Park on May 24, 1862. Teams were also forming in Victoria, and up-Island, where there were miners who had played the game in Britain.

Soccer was attractive because of the egalitarian nature of the game; it didn't matter whether a player was a product of the British public school system or had grown up in a Yorkshire mining town. All that was needed for the game were some willing players, sturdy boots, and a football.

Soccer, as the picture postcard suggests, was a popular game to mark holidays like the Queen's Birthday, Dominion Day, and Labour Day. While we do not know who won the New Denver/Sandon game played on May 24, 1906, doubtless it was enjoyed by play

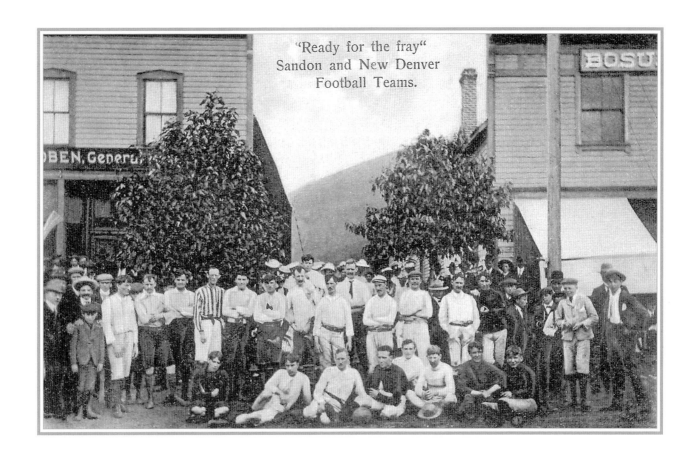

"Ready for the fray"
Sandon and New Denver
Football Teams.

THREE FORKS—SOON OUTCLASSED

In 1892, Eli Carpenter laid out a townsite between three creeks in the heart of the Silvery Slocan. He called his new town Three Forks. Initially, it could be reached only by wagon road from Kaslo or New Denver. However, in 1894 both the CPR's Nakusp and Sandon Railway and the Great Northern's narrow-gauge Kaslo and Sandon line reached Three Forks.

Soon the town had a population of over 2,000. The existence nearby of a concentrator that processed the rich local ore did much for Three Forks.

Still, by 1904 fewer than 400 were living in the town. The reason? Only four miles away another town, named Sandon, had come into being. It had not only running water and electric lights, but also 24 hotels and 23 saloons, stores, a bank, and a newspaper. There was just no way that Three Forks could compete with such amenities!

L. J. De Nobele, Import, Winnipeg

60 — Three Forks B. C.

SANDON—IN THE SILVERY SLOCAN

In the 1890s, Sandon was circled by silver and zinc mines. Life in Sandon wasn't easy for miners, who earned less than $3.50 per day. Most lived in hotels where room, board, and two whiskies a day cost a dollar. After buying clothes, paying life insurance and union dues, and sending something home to their families, they didn't have much left. Since the cost of living in Sandon was twice that of Ontario's and 25 percent higher than in mining camps south of the border, it is no surprise to learn that 80 percent of the miners were single.

Along with whores and Chinese laundrymen, these single men were generally not seen as true members of the community by the townsfolk. After all, miners were a transient lot. Transient or not, without their labour flash-in-the-pan towns like Sandon could not have existed, even for their few short years of prosperity, before they joined the growing number of ghost towns found today throughout British Columbia's Interior.

Sandon, British Columbia.

Published by Canada Drug and Book Co., Ltd., Nelson, British Columbia.

SANDON—A PACK TRAIN

Some old postcards have a narrative quality about them. It is as though they want to tell a tale, yet leave the telling of it to the viewer. One cannot help but wonder about the man and his pack train. He appears to be leaving Sandon as he passes under a flume and alongside some pioneer's cabin. But where is he going, and what about his freight?

Two of the horses are well burdened with chairs, while a third is loaded with a larger piece of furniture. And what about all those chairs? Are they on their way to a general store, or are they to furnish a new saloon somewhere in the Silvery Slocan? There is another possibility: perhaps the man is a peddler. Many an isolated prospector would have welcomed a peddler, not only because visitors were rarely seen, but because a store-bought chair, blanket, or table would have been a welcome and civilizing luxury in a cabin where everything else was homemade and looked it.

No one knows the real story the picture is telling, but it does seem to say something of toil, of discomfort, and of dreams yet to be fulfilled.

Pack Train
Sandon, B.C.

ROSSLAND—FATHER PAT'S MEMORIAL

Rossland is at the centre of a district where 50 percent of B.C.'s gold (worth $40 million by 1910) was mined before the First World War. Even though it had something of the roaring camp about it in the 1890s, Rossland was a community with heart. Its feelings are reflected in a somewhat bizarre monument erected on its main street. It serves man and beast with its drinking fountain, horse trough, and dogs' water dish. All it lacks is a birdbath!

It is a memorial to the Reverend Henry Irwin, an Irish Anglican priest known as Father Pat, who volunteered to serve as a missionary "in a country with a cold climate." Well, in B.C. he got his wish. He built churches and brought both the Gospel and welcome news of home to settlers, miners, and prospectors in many rough and isolated places throughout the Boundary District and Washington. As Father Pat put it, "the 49th parallel doesn't run through the Church." With failing health, the itinerant priest died at age 41 on his way home to Ireland. His memorial in Rossland suggests he didn't labour in vain.

"Father Pat" Memorial Fountain, Rossland, B. C.

TRAIL—A RELUCTANT CPR

Trail—originally Trail Creek Landing—is located at the point where the Dewdney Trail crossed the Columbia River. The original townsite was laid out in 1890 as a shipping point for the rich ore from the mines at nearby Rossland. In 1896, F. A. Heinze, a 24-year-old millionaire mining wizard from Butte, Montana, built a smelter at Trail to process ore from the Rossland mines. He also built the Columbia and Western Railway that linked the mines to his new smelter via 14 miles of dangerous twists and turns.

To the consternation of the CPR, Heinze's Columbia and Western charter also allowed him to build through to Penticton. He had, in fact, completed a line from Trail to West Robson in 1898. His move caught the CPR by surprise; it had been eying the route for its own Kettle Valley Railway. As it happened, the CPR got lucky; Heinze was involved in a legal battle with Standard Oil and Anaconda in Montana and wanted to sell his Canadian holdings. While the CPR happily bought his railway, it was not all that happy about being forced to buy his smelter as part of the $1-million deal.

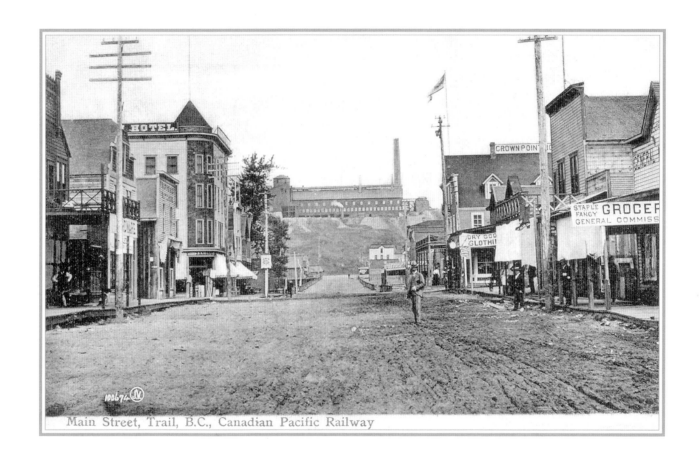

Main Street, Trail, B.C., Canadian Pacific Railway

NELSON—BAKER STREET

When Nelson was incorporated in 1897, it had a population of nearly 5,000 and was the largest city in Canada between Winnipeg and Vancouver. By 1910 the B.C. Directory was describing the city as "the administrative, commercial, industrial, mining, lumbering and fruit growing center [sic] of southeastern B.C." Nelson is unique, being much more the small city than the large town.

Perhaps its special appeal relates to Baker Street, with its two-and-a-half-mile streetcar line—the shortest street railway system in the British Empire. Then again, Nelson's special quality may relate to the fact that it was one of the few communities in B.C. never destroyed by fire. It has an abundance of first-rate heritage properties, including a number of stone buildings like the city hall, St. Saviour's Church, and a Frances Rattenbury-designed courthouse. And even though neither the CPR nor the Great Northern runs passenger trains into Nelson anymore, and there are no sternwheelers waiting at the dock, Nelson is still a great little city, full of character and charm.

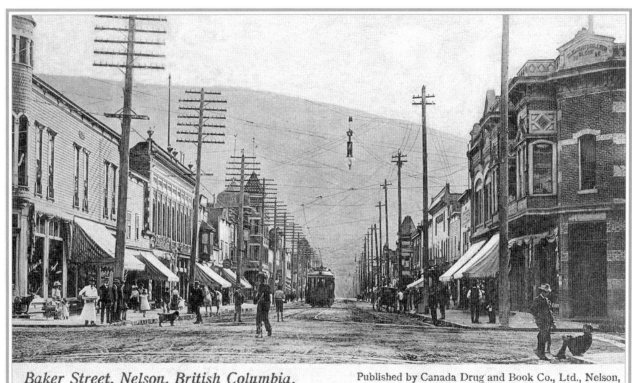

Baker Street, Nelson, British Columbia.

Published by Canada Drug and Book Co., Ltd., Nelson,
British Columbia.

KASLO—A GREAT NORTHERN TOWN

During the 1890s, when silver was king in the mountainous country that lies between the Arrow and Kootenay lakes, Kaslo was an important commercial centre. The town had a population of over 1,500 and at least 50 businesses, of which 20 were hotels and bars.

Kaslo was a Great Northern town. In 1895 the American railway's narrow-gauge Kaslo and Slocan Railway reached Sandon. The company hoped to siphon off the region's wealth to New York by way of Coeur d'Alene and Spokane. The CPR's Nakusp and Slocan Railway had made its way to Sandon in the same year.

In 1910, stiff competition and forest fires finished off the narrow-gauge line. The CPR took it over, converted it to standard gauge, and ran the full 59 miles between Nakusp and Kaslo until the line was abandoned in 1957.

And what of Kaslo today? Forestry, fruit farming, and the presence of the world's oldest surviving sternwheeler, the *Moyie*, have kept the town alive.

D.P.KANE.   FRONT STREET. KASLO. B.C.

85

POPLAR—PROSPECTORS AT WORK

In 1902, the CPR built the Kootenay and Arrowhead Railway. It ran from Lardeau at the north end of Kootenay Lake to Gerrard at the south end of Trout Lake. The line's name suggests there was hope that it might eventually be part of a longer line to Arrowhead and Revelstoke, where it would connect with the CPR's main line.

Less than a year after the railway was built, gold was discovered on its right-of-way at Poplar Creek. The strike, known as the Lucky Jack, soon had prospectors setting up camp and staking claims.

In no time at all a townsite came into being. It was not long before Poplar had a post office, four stores, six hotels, and seven saloons. Unfortunately, by the end of 1903 it was realized that the gold deposits were not nearly as rich as it was thought they would be. By 1909, Poplar's population was down to 50. Today little remains of the town that even had a newspaper for a few months in 1903— the *Poplar Creek Nugget*.

Prospectors Tent, Poplar, B. C.

CRESTON—THE MUNRO HOTEL

Creston lies in the valley of the Kootenay River at the centre of over 50,000 acres of rich farmland, much of it made available through a program of land reclamation. Before the First World War, over 50,000 acres were devoted to grain, strawberries, and tree fruits. The town, with a population of less than 1,000, had the only grain elevators in B.C. outside the Peace River district.

Like all small towns of the period, Creston's hotels relied heavily on the repeat visits of commercial travellers. Since salesmen spent much of their time on the road, hotels were always polishing their "home away from home" image to attract business. Creston's Munro Hotel ads let it be known that it had both "bath and toilet rooms" as well as hot and cold running water in all its rooms. The hotel also mentioned in its publicity that it had "Three Sample Rooms" where salesmen could display their goods. Still thinking of salesmen on the road, we find an interesting listing in the 1910 B.C. Directory for Minnie Williams' Amusement Parlour. Maybe there was more to Creston than met the eye! Then again, maybe not.

Creston, B. C.

89

MOYIE—A JULY-FIRST CELEBRATION

Moyie, 18 miles south of Cranbrook, was the site of the St. Eugene lead, silver and zinc mine. Holidays were a rare time for fun, and a century ago many places as close to the border as Moyie celebrated both July 1st and July 4th with parades, games, and good-natured friendly competition.

No holiday in small-town B.C. would have been complete without races, and a race that always attracted a crowd was the one that pitted the local volunteer hose company against a team from a neighbouring town. Hose companies literally pulled the hose reels to the site of a fire. In 1889, Vancouver's 15-man hose company became the North American Hose Team champions by defeating 12 American teams. The reels, with their oversized wheels, were for the most part manufactured by the Silby Company of Seneca Falls, New York. Hopefully, no one racing in Moyie needed medical attention; the local physician was Dr. J. W. Coffin.

Before the First World War the town had a population of over 1,200 people; today half that number live in Moyie.

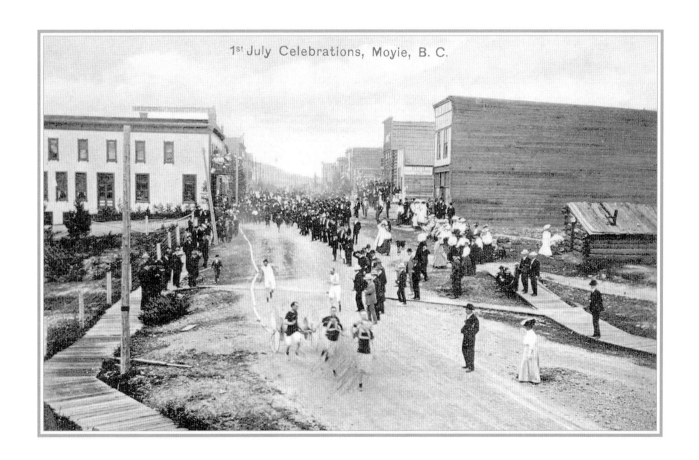

1st July Celebrations, Moyie, B. C.

ST. EUGENE—AN O.M.I. MISSION

By way of heritage, the Kootenay (Kutenai) Natives have more in common with the Natives of the prairies than they have with the coastal peoples, both in terms of appearance and lifestyle. The first mission to the Kutenai people was undertaken in 1874 by Father Leon Fouquet, a member of the French missionary Oblates of Mary Immaculate. Dedicated to St. Eugene, the mission station he established was 6 miles north of Cranbrook on the St. Mary's River.

In 1897, a beautiful church was built at the mission. Father Nicolas Coccola, an Oblate who spent 60 years in British Columbia, was much involved in the mining boom of the 1890s. He not only grubstaked the founder of the Sullivan mine at Kimberley, but was also a shareholder in Moyie's St. Eugene silver, zinc, and lead mine. It was the proceeds from the sale of his shares in the St. Eugene mine that paid for the church.

A residential industrial school accommodating 70 boarders opened at the St. Eugene Mission in 1912. Staffed by seven Sisters of Providence, it did not close until 1971.

Koofenay Indians St. Eugene Mission

CRANBROOK—JAMES BAKER'S CREATION

Cranbrook owes its existence to Colonel James Baker, who bought ranchland at Joseph's Prairie in 1886. He named his property Cranbrook Farm after his home in England. In the same year he was elected MLA for East Kootenay. He became Provincial Secretary and Minister of Education and Immigration in 1892, ands Minster of Mines as well in 1895. Baker's profitable involvement in coal mines near Fernie suggests his acceptance of the additional role in cabinet may not have been entirely altruistic.

The colonel did a number of interesting things. In 1897, he purchased a First Nations campground at Joseph's Prairie and had it surveyed, creating Cranbrook's townsite. As well, he encouraged the building of the CPR's Crowsnest Branch, and, most importantly, convinced the railway to run its line through Cranbrook rather than the highly favoured Fort Steele.

Baker left politics in 1898, retiring to England in 1900. The town he created prospered. The presence of over 700 CPR employees working both in and out of Cranbrook gave the community a stable basis for its century of growth.

No. 1317 — Main St., Cranbrook, B.C.

IMPERIAL BANK OF CANADA

WARDNER—IMPRESSIVE IN ITS DAY

Whenever British Columbia forests are mentioned, the picture that usually comes to mind is one of giant cedars and Douglas firs—the trees found in the coastal rain forest. It is easy to forget that lumbering has been, and still is, an important Interior industry.

Although Wardner is now a village of fewer than 200 people, it was once the site of an important East Kootenay mill town. The community, 16 miles southeast of Cranbrook, was created by an American, James T. Wardner, in 1895. His Crow's Nest Pass Lumber Company employed over 450 men. Prairie homesteaders formed a sizeable market for East Kootenay lumber, and a number of other mill towns like Wardner came into being. But by 1914, B.C.'s 800 logging camps and 400 mills, including those in the East Kootenay, were in poor shape; overproduction, freight costs, and shrinking domestic and overseas demand were all factors contributing to the downturn. But even before the First World War, the East Kootenay lumber industry was doomed for a generation; the area had already been "successfully" logged-off !

Saw Mill and Yards—C.N.P.L. Co., Ltd.—Wardner, B.C.

FERNIE—WINTER WHITE BEATS COAL-DUST BLACK

While coal had been discovered to the west of the Crow's Nest Pass (now Crowsnest) in 1873, it was not mined until the opening of the CPR's Crowsnest Pass line in 1898. Noted for its coking qualities, the coal was much in demand by smelters in British Columbia, Washington, and Idaho.

Much of Fernie, the region's chief town, was destroyed by fire on August 1, 1908. As is often the case, the forest fire that engulfed the town was both a bad news and a good news story. The destruction of the town was, of course, the bad news. The good news was that a better town was created, in which concrete and brick figured largely in the rebuilding.

The winter scene pictured has a certain Currier & Ives quality about it, suggesting a moment frozen in time. And what were all those people waiting to see as they stood looking into the street? While the answer is not known, the driver of the lone cutter must have felt a certain self-consciousness as he travelled along Fernie's Victoria Avenue that day.

Victoria Avenue looking North,
Fernie, B. C.

COAL CREEK—MINERS AND MINORS

Before the First World War, dangerous and unhealthy working conditions, poor pay, and little hope for the future was the lot of miners at Coal Creek, just as it was for coal miners everywhere. In 1897, adult miners were paid $3.50, labourers $2.25, and boys $1.00 a day. The soft coal mined at Coal Creek provided fuel for the railways and for local smelters. It had been hoped that the mines of the Crowsnest Pass would do for the province what the coalfields of Pennsylvania had done for that state.

In spite of the presence of the Coal Creek Literary and Athletic Association and the Methodist Church, life at Coal Creek was bleak and colourless. The uncontrolled liquor traffic, houses without proper foundations or plumbing, and hazardous working conditions created a community in which few, given the choice, would have lived. Of the many tears that were probably shed when the Coal Creek mine closed in 1958, doubtless few were of regret.

Miners at the Pit Mouth, Coal Creek, Fernie, B. C.

HOSMER—PARADISE LOST

Hosmer was one of a string of mining towns along the CPR's Crowsnest Pass division of what would become the railway's southern, or Kettle Valley, route to the coast in 1916. The town was also served by the Great Northern's Crowsnest Southern Railway. In 1909, with a population of 1,500, the town was right up there with the best of them. Hosmer Mines Limited employed 600 men and operated 240 coke ovens.

Thanks to the company, residents of Hosmer had electric light and running water. They also had two mail deliveries a day, a school, a hospital, several hotels (and bars), three churches, a bank, stores, and a weekly newspaper. Then, too, there was the Hosmer Opera House. What more could anyone ask? Today the town that once was is no better remembered than the man for whom it was named—C. R. Hosmer, one-time manager of CPR Telegraph and a director of the railway.

FRONT STREET, HOSMER, B. C.

103

THE CROWSNEST PASS—THE ROUTE TO KOOTENAY COAL

The Crownest Pass is the most southerly pass through the Canadian Rockies. In 1873, Michael Phillips, a trader and prospector, blazed a trail and became the first White person to use the Pass. The British Columbia Southern Railway, a CPR subsidiary, built a line through the Pass in 1897-98 to reach the rich East Kootenay coal deposits. The line was built from twelve miles east of the Pass to Kootenay Landing by Michael J. Haney (as in Haney, B.C.), using 5,000 men and 2,000 teams of horses.

In the years before the Great War, Andrew Good's Summit Hotel—or more accurately, its bar—was probably the social centre of the community (population, 31). While Good, who also owned the Crow's Nest Lime Works, was undoubtedly the village's leading citizen, it was also served by David Hughes' General Store and Post Office and was home to the offices of the McInnis Coal Company.

While the rail line is still very much in use, the only early CPR facility that remains is a 70-foot turntable that was used to turn snowplows around.

Crow's Nest, B. C.

FIELD—CLIMBING THE ROCKIES

The CPR's *Imperial Limited* is pictured at Field, having come down the four-mile-long Big Hill with its 4.5 percent grade between Hector and Mt. Stephen tunnel. In that the railway generally limited grades to a maximum of 2.2 percent, it is not surprising that there were three safety switches along the grade.

Trains travelling eastward could require as many as six locomotives to get them up through the 5,340-foot-high Kicking Horse Pass and across the Great Divide. Field was important not only because it was the turnaround point for the extra locomotives needed on the Big Hill, but also because it was one of the meal stops along the route through British Columbia. Because dining cars were particularly heavy pieces of rolling stock, they were not normally used in the mountains until the Big Hill was bypassed in 1909 by the Spiral Tunnels, which reduced the grade to an acceptable 2.2 percent.

Climbing the Rockies.

THE SPIRAL TUNNELS—BORN OF NECESSITY

The Big Hill began three miles west of the Continental Divide. It was the four-mile section of the CPR's original 1885 main line between Hector and Field. With an almost unheard of 4.5 percent grade, trains required four engines either for motive or braking power, and for safety's sake could only travel at four or five miles per hour.

To overcome the problem, between 1907 and 1909 tunnels were bored through two mountains. While these Spiral Tunnels increased the distance between Hector and Field by 4.5 miles, they reduced the grade to an acceptable 2.2 percent. Coming from the east, the new line passes through a 3,255-foot-long tunnel, curving 250 degrees under Cathedral Mountain. After crossing the Kicking Horse River, it enters a second 2,922-foot-long tunnel under Mount Ogden, circling 226 degrees before again crossing the Kicking Horse River.

The Spiral Tunnels cost approximately $1.5 million to build, and over 1,000 men were employed in their construction. Today, the abandoned Big Hill right-of-way serves as the route for the Trans-Canada Highway.

THE NEW AND THE OLD GRADE, FIELD, B.C.

ROGERS PASS—THE STATIONS

In February 1881, Major Albert B. Rogers was hired by the CPR to find a route that would allow the railway to build its main line through the Selkirk Mountains. Rogers discovered the pass that bears his name in May of the same year.

In 1885, a station was built at mile 85, site of the 4,275-foot summit construction camp. It was not long before a second "permanent" station, engine house, and bunkhouse were built farther east at mile 82.8. Eight people were killed when everything was swept away by an avalanche in January 1899.

A third station, roundhouse, and turntable were then built at mile 83.9. Beyond the avalanche area, there was a new problem: the yard's 1.6 percent grade was dangerously steep. In connection with a 1909 grade revision, a fourth station and a new water tank were built at mile 83.8. Snowfalls averaging 50 feet and severe slides forced the CPR to develop plans in 1910 for a tunnel under Rogers Pass. In 1916, the Connaught Tunnel was opened, and the more scenic, though hazardous, route through Rogers Pass was happily abandoned.

3176 - Mount Cheops from Rogers Pass, B. C.

Trueman Photo Vancouver B. C.

ROGERS PASS—SUMMER TRACKS

An unexpected cost associated with the construction of the CPR related to "winterproofing" the tracks through the mountain ranges of B.C. Snow in Rogers Pass caused the line to be closed over the winter of 1885-86. While William Van Horne, the CPR's general manager, knew that five miles of costly snowsheds would have to be built, he was also mindful of the fact that tourists would travel to B.C. not to spend their time inside snowsheds, but rather to enjoy the magnificent views along the right-of-way.

Van Horne ordered summer track to be laid along the outside of the 31 snowsheds in Rogers Pass so tourists could enjoy the spectacular scenery for a good part of the year. The sections of parallel summer and winter track between the snow sheds made selective routing possible; trains could be run through some sheds and outside others, depending on snow conditions. In summer, of course, the full length of summer track was used. Van Horne's call for both summer and winter tracks was a successful "have your cake and eat it too" way of solving the problem.

Train Outside Snowshed, Glacier, B. C.

GLACIER—THE CPR'S GLACIER HOUSE

Glacier House was one of the CPR's three original "Hotel Dining Stations" built to accommodate passengers. Dining cars were not used in the early years of the railway in B.C. because they were too heavy to be hauled up and down the steep mountain grades. The dining stop-cum-hotel stood at the foot of the Illecillewaet Glacier, giving it a special appeal for both experienced and would-be mountaineers.

Over the years, Glacier House was enlarged to the point where it eventually had 90 rooms, a billiard hall, swings, an observation tower with a large telescope, and a photographic darkroom for the use of guests. Interestingly, even though the hotel was located in a national park, it was advertised as being "a hunter's paradise of bear and goat." While Glacier House was bypassed with the opening of the Connaught Tunnel in 1916, its popularity was such that it remained open until 1925. It was the advent of the automobile and the CPR's consequent development of what were called Bungalow Camps that finally led to its closure.

Glacier House, Glacier, B. C.

115

ILLECILLEWAET—SWISS GUIDES LED THE WAY

Touted in the CPR's promotional material as the "Great Glacier of the Selkirks," Illecillewaet Glacier is near the summit of the Selkirks, the mountain range to the west of the Rockies. It was only two miles from the railway's hotel, Glacier House, which first opened in 1886.

In 1899 the railway had brought in Swiss guides to lead its hotel guests to the nearby glacier and adjacent mountain peaks. Potential climbers were told that although "there is no difficulty in reaching the foot of the glacier … and [that] it can be climbed to enjoy satisfying views of yawning crevasses and the vastness of the icefield," they would have to hire one of the company's Swiss guides and have spiked boots and thick gloves if they intended to venture any distance on the ice. While the fee to be paid Swiss guides was discreetly not mentioned, CPR brochures did let it be known that axes and ropes were supplied by the hotel without charge.

Ascending the Illecillewaet Glacier, B. C.

GOLDEN—THE STOLEN BELL

Golden is on the main line of the CPR. Like Cranbrook farther south, the town sits in the Rocky Mountain Trench, an 840-mile-long valley that lies between the Rockies and the Columbia, Omineca, and Cassiar ranges. Golden had all the amenities that one would expect to find in a B.C. small town a century ago—a school, a hospital, hotels, and businesses, the chief of which was the Columbia River Lumber Company.

The town also had the usual complement of churches, including St. Paul's Anglican Church with its stolen bell. It seems that a church building was being moved from Donald, a town on the CPR main line that had ceased to exist, to Windermere, where a church was needed. When the building's components were unloaded from flatcars at Golden to be loaded onto a barge that would carry them the 96 miles up the Columbia to Windermere, someone filched the bell for St. Paul's. To this day the "stolen" bell, originally donated by Baroness Angela Burdett-Coutts, a close friend of Queen Victoria, calls the faithful in Golden to worship Sunday by Sunday.

Golden, B. C.

REVELSTOKE—ON THE COLUMBIA

While most ships sailing B.C.'s inland waterways were owned by the CPR or the Great Northern, there were a few independently owned vessels. One was the *Revelstoke*.

Built at Nakusp for a group of Revelstoke businessmen, the ship was launched in 1902. It was designed for the 40 miles of treacherous water north from Revelstoke to Death Rapids on the Big Bend of the Columbia River. The 309-ton 125-foot-long sternwheeler only drew 22 inches of water. Its engines were designed to deliver more than double the horsepower of any ship that had previously plied the route. When sailing upstream, the *Revelstoke* consumed 42 cords of wood; while going downstream, only one cord of wood was burned.

Although the Big Bend goldfields were a thing of the past, prospectors still headed up north. Others travelling upriver were in search of green gold—timber. Loggers and sawmill equipment could usually be found aboard ship. The *Revelstoke* was laid up after 13 seasons. Its owners must have been well pleased with their excursion into steamboating.

4330   S. S. Revelstoke, Columbia River Canyon, B. C.   Trueman Photo, Vancouver, B. C.

SICAMOUS—A SHINGLED CHATEAU

Sandwiched between the railway tracks and Shuswap Lake, the CPR's station-hotel at Sicamous was built in 1897 to replace the original depot that had been destroyed by fire. It was built primarily to serve as a layover station for passengers who were connecting with the local train to or from Okanagan Landing. Its location also made it a favourite with honeymooners as well as fishermen and boaters.

The building was designed by Edward Maxwell, who created a number of first-class stations and hotels for the CPR. As pictured, the original shingled station-hotel with its central pavilion and polygonal turrets was in the railway's signature Chateau style. The building was enlarged to double its size in 1910 and transmogrified into a Tudor half-timbered structure. The 75-room hotel closed in 1957 when passenger service to the Okanagan was discontinued. The old building's life wasn't quite finished, however, in that it continued to be a station until 1964, when it was demolished.

Sicamous Hotel & Lake.

SALMON ARM—PICTURE-PERFECT

Salmon Arm is located on the south arm of Shuswap Lake. While it is at the heart of a region noted for dairy farms, orchards, and lumbering, it is not a town with a wildly interesting past. At the beginning of the twentieth century, it had the usual complement of churches and secret societies. In addition to the Canadian Order of Chosen Friends and other lodges, there were the Masons, who held their meetings on "the first Wednesday evening on or before the full moon."

While Salmon Arm "way back when" doesn't seem all that special, the picture postcard of the town's wharf is superb. The swaybacked sternwheeler is visually balanced by the team of swaybacked horses, and somehow the roofline of the shed at the centre of the picture matches up geometrically with the roofline on the left of the picture. As well, the stillness that pervades the scene gives the picture a surreal or dreamlike quality. Salmon Arm may have been a rather ordinary place, but the postcard produced for sale by W. E. Pratt, the town's druggist, stationer, and veterinary surgeon, is certainly way above average.

The Wharf, Salmon Arm, B. C.

KELOWNA—POLO

Polo was first played in Victoria in 1889 when officers of the Royal Navy challenged "the sporting gentlemen of Victoria" to a game. While polo had limited appeal on the coast, it quickly took hold in southern Alberta. There, British younger sons, whom the *Calgary Herald* described as "too lazy to plow and too shiftless to own cattle," formed polo clubs in Calgary, Pincher Creek, High River, and Fort Macleod.

In B.C., the first mention of an Interior team was in 1896 when a Nicola Valley four played in a tournament in Victoria. A polo club was formed in Kamloops in 1897, and its members played regularly against Westwold. By 1900, polo clubs were being established in Vernon, Coldstream, and Kelowna, which, of course, had plenty of remittance men for whom polo was just the game! After the Great War the Vernon and Coldstream clubs amalgamated, playing on into the 1930s. The Kelowna Club did not survive the war that saw so many young men march off to die for King and Country. If only the casualties had been of as little consequence as polo.

Polo at Kelowna, B. C.

KELOWNA—TOBACCO ROAD

While thoughts of the Okanagan usually conjure visions of fruit trees and wineries, there was a time when Kelowna was also home to a successful, if short-lived, tobacco industry. The first experimental crop was planted in 1894 by L. H. Holman of Wisconsin. He interested others in developing a tobacco industry, and in March 1912 they incorporated the British North American Tobacco Company.

Seed imported from Cuba was sown in April in frames protected from frost by cheesecloth and canvas covers. The plants were transplanted to the open fields by the last week in May. Pure Cuban tobacco was grown for "filler," Constock Spanish Wisconsin for "binders," and high-quality Sumatran for wrappers. The harvested tobacco was cured in specially constructed barns.

There were at least two cigar factories in Kelowna producing over 130,000 cigars a month. The industry did not last, however; other countries could produce a finer tobacco and market it at a lower price than could the enthusiastic entrepreneurs of Kelowna.

COPYRIGHT 1909
G.H.E. HUDSON
KELOWNA B.C.

MR. HOLMAN'S TOBACCO HARVEST, KELOWNA, B.C.

SUMMERLAND—FRUIT RANCHING ON THE LAKE

Before the First World War, roads in the Okanagan were either terrible or non-existent. Most communities like Summerland relied on the CPR's lake boats for access to the outside world and its barge service to get their boxes of fruit and cases of canned fruit and vegetables to market.

In 1910, Summerland's 800 inhabitants were served by four churches, a bank, a hospital, a Baptist college, and the usual main street stores and offices. It also had a brass band and baseball, cricket, and canoe clubs. Looking after business were the Farmers' Institute and the Board of Trade. The *Summerland Review,* the Lake Shore Telephone Company, and the CPR Telegraph kept the citizens of Summerland in touch with the world.

The CPR's *Okanagan*, launched in 1907, is pictured at the wharf in Summerland, together with loaded freight cars waiting for a tug and transfer barge to carry them to Okanagan Landing and the line to Sicamous, where they will be moved either east or west along the CPR's main line.

Summerland, B. C.

PENTICTON—THE SOFT-FRUIT TOWN

Penticton took its name from a cattle ranch pre-empted by Thomas Ellis in 1866. In 1905, the Southern Okanagan Land Company bought a sizeable tract of land from Ellis, created a townsite, and encouraged the development of a commercial tree-fruit industry. Penticton grew quickly and on January 1, 1909, was incorporated as a district municipality with a population of 900. It soon had a four-room school, a nursing home, a bank, shops, three hotels, and a telephone company able to "provide long-distance communication to points as far away as Kamloops."

Transportation in and out of town was either by lake steamer to Okanagan Landing and the CPR or by stagecoach to Oroville, Washington, there to connect with a Great Northern line to Spokane.

Penticton became a city in 1948 and has a population today of over 30,000. Ellis didn't do badly either; after he had sold off all his ranchlands he was a wealthy man, well able to retire in style to Victoria.

KAMLOOPS—ONE OF B.C.'S OLDEST TOWNS

While Kamloops may have been one of the Interior's principal cities in the 1890s, it still had a frontier look about it. Pictured at its moorings near cordwood waiting to be used to fire its boilers is the *Kamloops*. Incredibly, such sternwheelers navigated over 900 miles along the Thompson/Shuswap waterways. And running along the town's main street are the CPR's tracks. Even though the first train arrived in Kamloops in November 1885, the riverboats continued to operate for years, serving the orchardists and truck gardeners along the riverbank flatlands, as well as cattle ranchers along the tablelands and in the valleys.

Kamloops has a long history. In 1812, David Stuart established a fur-trading post at the confluence of the North and South Thompson rivers for Jacob Astor's Pacific Fur Company. The North West Company bought out Pacific Fur in 1813, and was itself taken over by the Hudson's Bay Company in 1821. It was the railway that in time transformed what had been little more than a trading post into the important centre Kamloops is today.

Kamloops, B. C.   On C. P. R.

KAMLOOPS—THE RESIDENTIAL SCHOOL

While Native residential schools are cause for apology on the part of White society that brought them into being, in their day they were regarded as appropriate and progressive. There were seventeen such schools in B.C., ten of them Roman Catholic. Within the Roman Church, the Durieu System, as it came to be called, gave form to a particular perspective.

Paul Durieu, Bishop of New Westminster and Vicar Apostolic in B.C., developed a strict system of social control intended not only to Christianize the Natives, but also to obliterate all vestiges of their centuries-old culture. Residential schools, in which children removed from their home environment were brought up as good Christian "European" young people, were a legitimate part of the "system." The residential school in Kamloops opened in 1890.

In the residential schools, the children's active involvement in marking special times in the Christian year was seen as particularly important. None was more elaborately staged than the Holy Week re-enactment of Christ's Passion.

Passion Play, Indian Reserve, Kamloops, B.C.

TRANQUILLE—AN IDEAL SETTING

For more than 50 years, victims of tuberculosis were treated at Tranquille on Kamloops Lake. In 1907, when the sanitarium opened in ranch buildings remodelled to accommodate 25 patients, the only path to recovery called for rest, a healthy diet, and fresh, clean, dry air, such as is found in B.C.'s dry belt. And because as was discovered in 1882, TB is caused by bacterial infection, isolation of the highly contagious patients at a centre like Tranquille was very important.

In 1910, a new main building was erected and the provincial TB hospital became known as the King Edward Sanitarium. Designed by Vancouver architect W. T. Dalton, the vaguely Arts and Crafts building was well suited and well sited to serve as a "fresh air hospital" for those suffering from TB. Dalton generously turned over his $3,500 fee to the Tuberculosis Society and met all his own travel expenses. The building was opened by Lieutenant-Governor T. W. Paterson.

Sanitarium, Tranquille, B. C.

QUESNEL—AT THE CENTRE OF THINGS

Quesnel had its beginning in 1863 as Quesnellmouth, at the confluence of the Quesnel and Fraser rivers. Its name honoured Jules Maurice Quesnel, a North West Company fur trader who travelled with Simon Fraser in 1808 as he explored the river that bears his name. Quesnel didn't last long in the Cariboo; after only three years in New Caledonia (northern B.C.), he described the territory as "misery and boredom" and returned to Montreal and a successful career in business and politics. Regardless, the community known as Quesnel took on a life of its own. Gold had been discovered in the Cariboo in the early 1860s, and the town developed as the supply centre for mines and miners in the region.

By 1865, Quesnel had a number of stores and a hotel close to the town's steamboat landing. The hotel was the Occidental. In spite of its "Queen Anne in front, and just plain Mary Anne behind" look, it was regarded as the best hotel along the Cariboo Wagon Road. In 1907, the hostelry was sold to Edward Kepner of Seattle. He soon razed the "historic" building, erecting an opulent new four-storey hotel.

Occidental Hotel,
Quesnel, B.C.

141

FRASER LAKE—THE GRAND TRUNK PACIFIC

Built between 1905 and 1914, the Grand Trunk Pacific was a 2,982-mile rail line that ran between Winnipeg and Prince Rupert by way of the Yellowhead Pass. It was the brainchild of C. M. Hayes, president of the Grand Trunk Railway, a significant line in Ontario and Quebec.

The route along the Skeena River between Prince Rupert and Kitselas was particularly difficult to build, and over 5,000 tons of explosives were used to create the right-of-way for this relatively short section of the line.

By the time the last spike was driven at Finmore near Fort Fraser on April 7, 1914, the new railway's future was already looking bleak. Hayes had gone down with the *Titanic* in 1912, the depression of 1912-13 had seriously reduced revenue, and the outbreak of the First World War closed off access to much-needed foreign capital. The Grand Trunk Pacific went into receivership in 1919 and was taken over by the federal government.

Linking up of Steel on G. T. P. Transcontinental 1914.

HAZLETON—NORTHERN PACK TRAINS

Hazleton is at the confluence of the Skeena and Bulkley rivers. Laid out in 1871, the townsite is adjacent to an old Gitksan village.

Pack trains were a common sight in Hazleton a century ago. Beyond the town, the Skeena River ceases to be navigable, and all goods destined for points farther east or to the north had to be carried by pack animals over primitive trails. Some were created by the Collins Overland Telegraph Company when it was building an overland link between North America and Europe by way of Alaska and Siberia. By 1866, the line had passed through Hazleton and gone on to Telegraph Creek. The project came to a grinding halt in the same year when it was learned that the Atlantic cable had been laid successfully.

The discovery of gold in 1869 on the tributaries of the Omenica River and at Cassiar in 1874 led to short bouts of gold fever. Farther north, "B.C.'s last gold rush" began near Atlin in 1898. All these gold strikes, major and minor, meant work for the pack trains that quite literally were the lifeline for many living in northern British Columbia 100 years ago.

PACK TRAIN RETURNING, HAZELTON, B.C.

THE STIKINE—A NORTHERN RIVER

In 1897 gold was discovered in the Yukon. The easiest route to the goldfields was by way of Skagway, the Chilcoot Pass, and the Yukon River. But the government wanted an all-Canadian route to the diggings or, more accurately, an almost all-Canadian route via the Stikine River, which has its final 30 miles in U.S. territory.

The CPR chartered steamers, built river boats, and, it was assumed, would be building a connecting rail line from Glenora on the Skeena to Teslin in the Yukon. But things didn't work out. The Senate defeated a bill calling for money to be spent on a railway, and the route via Skagway, providing relatively easier access to the Klondike, became "the only way to go."

After only three months the CPR discontinued its Stikine River service, which was just as well since the land route from Glenora to Lake Teslin was mostly muskeg, mud, and mosquitoes. The all-Canadian route was soon to become no more than a bad memory.

101, Gasoline River Boat "Telegraph" ascending Stikine River.

TELEGRAPH CREEK—GATEWAY TO THE NORTH

I n 1900, there were not many places in B.C. that were either too small or too remote to have at least one picture postcard for sale featuring a local view. Even Telegraph Creek with its 200 people, both White and Native, had postcards for sale. Telegraph Creek, about 150 miles upstream from Wrangell, Alaska, was, and still is, the only town on the Stikine River. It is at the head of navigation, just below what is known as the Grand Canyon of the Stikine, and had its beginning with the discovery of gold in 1861.

In 1866, the Collins Overland Telegraph Company's line reached the town—hence its name—and gave it a new, if short-lived, lease on life. The community continues to exist principally because it is a point of contact with the outside world for those who chose to search for their fame and fortune in the sparsely settled north. The town's post office opened over a century ago, on July 1, 1899, and is still functioning. Perhaps there are still people in Telegraph Creek writing postcards that read, "Having wonderful time, wish you were here."

11817. Telegraph Creek, B. C.

Published by W. H. Case, Juneau, Alaska.

TELEGRAPH CREEK—TAHLTAN CHILDREN

Although no one moved a muscle a century ago when being photographed, the Tahltan children pictured were doing more than keeping still. Their demeanour was saying that all was not sweetness and light in their lives. But how could it have been when they were being dressed and educated as bronze-skinned little White children?

The drainage basin of the upper Stikine River was the traditional land of the Tahltan people for centuries before White prospectors arrived in their territory in 1861. Although they speak an Athapascan dialect, the Tahltan had close contact with the coastal Tlingit. They long ago adopted their potlatch, totemic brotherhoods (Tahltan are either Raven or Wolf), and the principle of heredity through the female line.

Even though the Tahltan's contact with Europeans was late, it was disastrous: smallpox epidemics of 1864 and 1868 reduced a tribe of over 1,000 people to fewer than 200 by 1900. Today the Tahltan number about 800, and hopefully their children have more to look forward to in life than did the youngsters pictured in a postcard nearly a century ago.

Tahl-tan Indian children.

THE STIKINE GLACIER—BACK OF BEYOND

The Stikine Glacier is found in the southeast corner of Spatsizi Plateau Wilderness Provincial Park, which is 195 miles north of Hazleton. Perhaps more amazing than the postcard picturing the Stikine Glacier is the fact that nearly a century ago someone managed to make his way to the remote glacier, carting along the incredibly cumbersome and heavy photographic equipment of the day. That someone was J. Howard A. Chapman of Victoria.

Born in England, Chapman settled in Victoria in 1890, where he found employment as a commercial traveller. Where and when he acquired his outstanding photographic skills is unknown. It is known, however, that his first series of B.C. postcards was published before 1906, and that he had produced over 700 different postcards by 1910. It has been suggested that Chapman took his pictures, later published as postcards, during his days as a travelling salesman, when he had to spend time waiting for retailers or transportation. By 1917 Chapman had become a full-time commercial photographer, though he produced few postcards in his latter years.

The Stickene Glacier.

PINE CREEK—B.C.'S LAST GOLD RUSH

I n January 1896, Fritz Miller and Kenneth Mclaren set off from Juneau, Alaska, in search of gold that was rumoured to have been found on the east side of Atlin Lake. They hiked over the White Pass from Skagway north to Bennett, where they left the Klondike Trail, heading east. After crossing snow-covered mountains and frozen lakes, they arrived on the eastern shore of Atlin Lake at a point about 96 miles due east of Skagway. They found shallow deposits in a rivulet they named Pine Creek. Out of provisions, they made their way back to Juneau, returning in the summer with six other men. They staked their claims on Pine Creek, six miles north of present-day Atlin, and began placer mining. Fritz Miller picked up $120 worth of gold on his first day on Pine Creek.

Word spread, and by the close of 1898 over 3,000 were working the streams and creeks. By 1900, the placer miners had to compete with hydraulic mining companies. As well, a bucket dredge, which was an expensive failure, was at work on Pine Creek. However, by 1903 hydraulic mining companies had won the day. Placer mining was finished.

Mining on Pine Creek, Atlin B. C.

No. 204 Publ. Atlas Society 10 E. 23. St. New York. Made in Germany.

ATLIN—IN THE CORNER POCKET

Not far below the Yukon border in the remote northwest corner of B.C. is Atlin. The town is a mining community with a population of about 500 people. In 1900, only four years after gold had been discovered in nearby Pine Creek, it had a population of over 5,000.

Even though Atlin was an isolated tent city in 1898, it wasn't long before things changed. Real-estate men were on the scene by 1899 laying our town lots, and there were three sawmills in operation. The school opened in a large tent in November 1899. Half the floor was planked and half was sawdust. A proper schoolhouse wasn't built until 1902. Although the town had a telegraph line to Dawson City and Skagway in 1899, as well as a local telephone system, it was not until 1903 that the B.C. Power and Manufacturing Co. bought Skagway's old power plant, moved it to Atlin, and supplied the town with electricity. By then, however, Atlin had changed. The get-rich-quick boys had left town, and the ongoing search for gold was left to the big companies with their sophisticated and efficient hydraulic equipment.

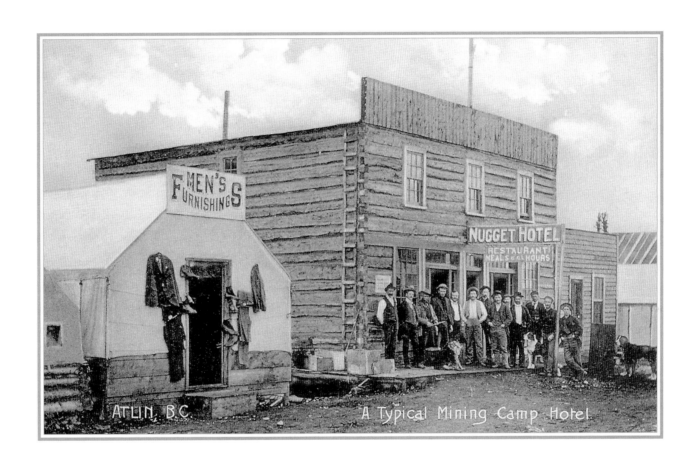

MEN'S FURNISHINGS

NUGGET HOTEL
RESTAURANT
MEALS S a.l HOURS

ATLIN, B.C.   A Typical Mining Camp Hotel.

PORT SIMPSON—A COMMUNITY WITH A MISSION

Fort Simpson (originally Fort Naas) was established by the Hudson's Bay Company on the Naas River in 1830 to protect its interests in the presence of Russian and American fur traders. The site was less than ideal, and in 1834 the trading post was relocated to the coast. Along the way Fort Simpson became Port Simpson, and by 1840 over 2,000 Tsimshian had come to live alongside the HBC's post.

In 1874, Thomas Crosby, a Methodist missionary, began his 23-year ministry among the Natives. He insisted that they abandon their heathen practices and adopt a Western way of life. By the mid-1880s, European-style housing had replaced longhouses, and soon a church, school, hospital, Boys' Home, and Girls' Home were added to the community.

The Grand Trunk Pacific's creation of the new town of Prince Rupert led to the decline of Port Simpson as the centre of commerce on the North Coast. Nevertheless, with a population of over 1,200 Natives, Port Simpson is still one of the largest and most important Native communities in the province.

Indian Village, Port Simpson, B. C.

METLAKATLA—ONE MAN'S DREAM

Metlakatla is a North Coast Tsimshian village. In 1862 William Duncan, Anglican lay minister at Port Simpson, moved with 400 of his converts to the old village to establish a utopian Native community. Duncan was charismatic, energetic, and autocratic. He banned liquor and the giving away of belongings at potlatches and expected children to go to school and adults to receive religious instruction and to be clean, industrious, and peaceful. He established a sawmill and a cannery and introduced loom weaving. He also chose 20 elders for the church and 20 uniformed Native constables to maintain law and order.

But all was not peace and light in this Garden of Eden. Duncan fought with both the civil and the church authorities and shared little real power with the Natives. Finally in 1888, with the blessing of the U.S. government, he moved with 800 of his followers to Alaska's Annette Island, where he established New Metlakatla, which survives to this day.

Indian Jail, Metlatkla.

THE SKEENA—A LIFE-GIVING RIVER

The Skeena is the second-longest river entirely within British Columbia. Over the centuries, its annual salmon run has provided sustenance for First Nations people. As well, when commercial fisheries came on the scene in the late 19th century, one-third of the province's commercial fishing fleet was either owned or crewed by Native people, for whom the fisheries became an important source of income. On northern rivers like the Skeena, a far greater percentage of those fishing for salmon were Native, and fully one-quarter of the salmon caught in B.C. waters in 1900 were taken from the Skeena River.

The first salmon cannery on the Skeena was the Inverness Cannery, which went into operation in 1876. Salmon canning was a labour-intensive industry, and it was both local Natives and Chinese brought from Vancouver for the canning season who got the job done 100 years ago. While other industries have become economically more important over the years, the annual salmon catch still provides a significant source of income for those fishing on the Skeena.

Salmon Fishing, Skeena River B. C.

PRINCE RUPERT—"IF ONLY ..."

There is something wonderfully incongruous about a fish market featuring a display of deer carcasses. But then, the postcard is from Prince Rupert, a town with a difference. Incorporated on March 3, 1910, Prince Rupert was the creation of one man, Charles M. Hayes, president of the Grand Trunk Pacific. Hayes chose a rock-solid island, much of which had to be blasted away, to be the western terminus and townsite for his railway. A contest was held to find a name for the new city and Prince Rupert won out.

Prince Rupert's story is very much an "if only" story—if only Hayes hadn't gone down with the *Titanic*, if only the federal government had continued to guarantee the railway's bonds, if only the Great War hadn't closed world markets. If only, if only, if only ...! By 1919, the Grand Trunk Pacific had to declare bankruptcy, forcing the federal government to take it over and ultimately combine its assets with those of other bankrupt railways to create the Canadian National system. Meanwhile, Prince Rupert developed an important fishing industry and managed to survive its darkest days between the two world wars.

PRINCE RUPERT FISH MARKET.

Deer shot in the vicinity of Prince Rupert, B. C.

PRINCE RUPERT—DREAMS AND REALITY

On May 17, 1906, the building of Prince Rupert began. The Grand Trunk Pacific's 2,000-acre townsite was realtors' heaven! So much so that by 1909 there were 32 realty firms trying to cash in on the bonanza. While salesmen dreamt of streets of gold, the reality was quite different.

The province spent $20,000 on preliminary improvements, and, as the B.C. Directory reported, "the greater part ... was expended on sidewalks and roadways, sewers, and water mains." Streets were planked to a width of 24 feet and had wooden sidewalks four feet wide. The water supply had the potential to supply the needs of a population of 200,000. Rails ran up Centre Street so that carloads of building materials and equipment could be winched over and up the steep and very rough grade by a donkey engine.

It wasn't long before dreams of 200,000 evaporated. In 1919, the Grand Trunk Pacific had to declare bankruptcy, and by 1933, the City of Prince Rupert was also bankrupt. The city had to wait until after the Second World War for better times when at least a few of its dreams would be matched by reality.

CENTRE STREET PRINCE RUPERT B.C.

1563

PORT ESSINGTON—JUST A MEMORY

Robert Cunningham came to B.C. in 1862 to assist William Duncan at Metlakatla. By 1867, he had decided the missionary life was not for him, and he went to work for the Hudson's Bay Company. In 1870, together with a partner, he established a trading post on the south shore of the Skeena estuary, which he named Port Essington.

The village grew even though it was only accessible by water. Cunningham established a salmon cannery in 1883, and by the early 1890s three other canneries were also in operation. The village soon became the transfer point for those who had come up the coast by steamer and wanted to continue up the Skeena River by sternwheeler.

Between 1906 and 1910, while the Grand Trunk Pacific was under construction, Port Essington flourished economically. Unfortunately, the completion of the railway to its terminus in Prince Rupert on the north side of the Skeena's estuary brought on Port Essington's slow but steady decline. The last cannery closed in 1936, and what was left of the deserted village was destroyed by a forest fire in 1957.

Port Essington B. C., Dufferin Street

MASSET—THE HAIDA NATION

Old Masset is on the north shore of Graham Island in the Queen Charlotte Islands, the ancestral home of the Haida. It is near present-day Masset, which was established in 1907. The old village was one of two to which the remaining Haida came to live in the later 19th century after European diseases like scarlet fever and smallpox had decimated their population. The first Europeans to make contact with the Haida were Spanish explorers who arrived on the Pacific Coast in 1774.

The Haida were an energetic nation. Their ocean-going canoes could carry as many as 60 of their warriors. Using these craft, they were able to raid villages from Alaska to Puget Sound for slaves and plunder. While they were formidable warriors, the Haida were also a creative and talented people. They built huge longhouses and carved house poles that were often 50 to 60 feet high. The last old totem pole raised in the Queen Charlotte Islands was at Old Masset in 1884. While the Haida nation was reduced to fewer than 600 a century ago, today its 3,500 people are proudly reclaiming their rich Native heritage.

TOTEM POLES, Massett, Q. C. Island.

T. N. Hibben & Co., Victoria B. C.

SAILING THE COAST—GOING HOME

It has been said that what goes up must come down. While this is not always true when it is "up north" and "down south" that is being spoken of, comparatively few non-Natives spent their lives in northern B.C. Sooner or later, most who went up north came down south again to Vancouver, Victoria, or wherever it was they called home. Every year a great many prospectors, placer miners, and those working for hydraulic mining companies headed south before winter. As well, the non-Native cannery workers, most of whom were Chinese, returned to the city once the summer's work was over. It could be said that those who wintered in the north either had very good reason for doing so or didn't have the money to pay for the trip down the coast.

The CPR's *Princess Royal*, a ship built in B.C. Marine Railway's Esquimalt Yard in 1907, provided a luxurious way to travel down the coast. While the *Princess Royal* could pitch and toss and, having a wooden hull, could "undulate like a centipede," what was a little shimmy and shake for those lucky enough to be going home?

11901. C. P. R. Steamer "Princess Royal."

Published by W. H. Case, Juneau, Alaska.

SELECTED BIBLIOGRAPHY

Anderson, W.A. *Cranbrook Heritage Report*. Cranbrook: Cranbrook Archives, Museum and Landmark Foundation, 1979.

Ashwell, Reg. *Indian Tribes of the Northwest*. Saanichton: Hancock House, 1977.

Barrett, Anthony A. and R.W. Liscombe. *Francis Rattenbury and British Columbia*. Vancouver: University of British Columbia Press, 1983.

Basque, Garnet. *Ghost Towns & Mining Camps of the Boundary Country*. Surrey: Heritage House (first edition), 1999.

——. *West Kootenay: The Pioneer Years*. Surrey: Heritage House, 1990.

Bilsland, William W. "Atlin 1898-1910; The Story of a Gold Boom." *B.C. Historical Quarterly* Vol. 16, Number 3-4 (1952): 121-179

Boam, Henry J. with Ashley G. Brown. *British Columbia*. London: Sells, 1912.

Burrows, Roger G. *Railway Mileposts: British Columbia, Vol. I, The CPR Mainline Route*. North Vancouver: Railway Mileposts, 1981.

——. *Railway Mileposts: British Columbia, Vol. II, The Southern Routes*. North Vancouver: Railway Mileposts, 1984.

Downs, Art. *Paddlewheels on the Frontier*. Seattle: Superior Publishing, 1972.

Francis, Daniel. *Encyclopedia of British Columbia*. Madeira Park: Harbour Publishing, 2000.

Gosnell, R.E. *The Year Book of British Columbia*. Victoria: Legislative Assembly, 1901.

——. *The Year Book of British Columbia*. Victoria: Legislative Assembly, 1911.

Hacking, N.R. and W. Kaye Lamb. *The Princess Story: A Century and a Half of West Coast Shipping*. Vancouver: Mitchell Press, 1974.

Hart, E. J. *The Selling of Canada*. Banff: Altitude Publishing, 1983.

Harvey, R.G. *Carving the Western Path: By River, Rail and Road Through B.C.'s Southern Mountains*. Surrey: Heritage House, 1998.

——. *Carving the Western Path: By River, Rail and Road through Central and Northern B.C.* Surrey: Heritage House, 1999.

Henderson's British Columbia Gazetteer and Directory for 1910. Vancouver: Henderson Publishing, 1910.

Isenor, D.E., W.N. McInnis, E.G. Stephens, D.E. Wilson. *Land of Plenty*. Campbell River: Ptarmigan Press, 1987.

Johnson, Patricia M. *Nanaimo*. North Vancouver: Trendex Publications, 1974.

Kenney, Jim with Sport B.C. *Champions: A British Columbia Sports Album*. Vancouver: Douglas & McIntyre, 1985.

Large, R. Geddes. *The Skeena: River of Destiny*. Surrey: Heritage House, 1996.

Lavallee, Omar. *Van Horne's Road*. Montreal: Railfare Enterprises, 1974.

Leechman, Douglas. *Native Tribes of Canada*. Toronto: W.J. Gage, 1956.

MacDonald, Robert. *The Uncharted Nations: Canada III*. Calgary: The Ballantrae Foundation, 1978.

Norton, Wayne. *A Whole Little City by Itself: Tranquille and Tuberculosis*. Kamloops: Plateau Press, 1999.

Paterson, T.W. *Ghost Town Trails of Vancouver Island*. Langley: Stage Coach Publishing, 1975.

Peake, Frank A. *The Anglican Church in British Columbia*. Vancouver: Mitchell Press, 1959.

Resorts in the Canadian Rockies. Montreal: Canadian Pacific Railway Hotel System, 1908.

Robinson, J. Lewis and Walter G. Hardwick. *British Columbia: One Hundred Years of Geographical Change*. Vancouver: Talon Books, 1973.

Schroeder, Andreas. *Carved From Wood: Mission, B.C., 1861-1992*. Mission: The Mission Foundation, 1991.

Segger, Martin. *Victoria: A Primer for Regional History in Architecture, 1843-1929*. Victoria: Heritage Architectural Guides, 1979.

Stacey, Susan. *Salmonopolis: The Steveston Story*. Madeira Park: Harbour Publishing, 1994.

Stevensen, John. "William Duncan: Missionary to the Tsimshian." *Frontier Days in British Columbia*, Garnet Basque, ed. Surrey: Heritage House, 2000.

Taylor, G.W. *Shipyards of British Columbia: The Principal Companies* Victoria: Morriss Publishing, 1986.

——. *Timber*. North Vancouver: J.J. Douglas, 1975.

Turnbull, Elsie. *Ghost Towns and Drowned Towns of West Kootenay*. Surrey: Heritage House, 1988.

Turner, Robert D. *Sternwheelers and Steam Tugs*. Victoria: Sono Nis Press, 1984.

——. *The Pacific Princesses*. Victoria: Sono Nis Press, 1977.

Whitehead, Margaret. *The Cariboo Mission: A History of the Oblates*. Victoria: Sono Nis Press, 1981.

Yesake, M. and Harold and Kathy Steves. *Steveston:Cannery Row*. Richmond: Self-published, 1998.

INDEX